Crystals for Life

BY

JACQUIE BURGESS

PHOTOGRAPHS BY

GILLIAN BUCKLEY

Newleaf

Newleaf
an imprint of
Gill & Macmillan Ltd
Hume Avenue, Park West
Dublin 12
with associated companies throughout the world
www.gillmacmillan.ie

© *2000 Jacquie Burgess*
0 7171 2888 1
Index compiled by Helen Litton
Print origination by Carole Lynch
Printed in Malaysia

The paper used in this book comes from the wood pulp of managed forests. For every tree felled, at least one tree is planted, thereby renewing natural resources.

A catalogue record is available for this book
from the British Library.

5 6 4

Contents

Introduction   vii

Section I: AN INTRODUCTION TO CRYSTALS   1
  1. The Crystal Healing Tradition   3
  2. The Physical Properties of Crystals   10
  3. How to Choose Crystals   16
  4. Caring for your Crystals   24
  5. How Crystals can Improve your Life   33

Section II: CRYSTALS IN THE HOME   47
  6. Crystal Healing   49
  7. Crystals and Communal Living   63
  8. Crystals and Personal Space   79
  9. Crystals for Children   88

Section III: CRYSTALS AT WORK   99
  10. Travelling   101
  11. The Workplace   108
  12. Concentration and Inspiration   119

Section IV: CRYSTALS IN THE GARDEN   127
  13. Crystal Gardening   129
  14. Gardens to Refresh the Spirit   139
  15. Sacred Circles   153

Section V: CRYSTALS AND INNER SPACE   171
  16. Crystal Dreaming   173
  17. Crystals and Meditation   180

18. Crystals, Visualisation and Inner Journeys   194
19. Meditation with Sound and Movement   203

Section VI: COLOUR CRYSTAL DIRECTORY   211
   Black Stones   216
   Red, Orange and Peach Stones   219
   Yellow and Gold Stones   225
   Green Stones   228
   Blue and Turquoise Stones   234
   Indigo and Violet Stones   240
   White, Pink and Rutilated Stones   244

Reference Notes   256
Recommended Reading   257
Acknowledgments   262
Further Information   263
Index   264

To Herbie
my love

Introduction

The times have certainly been a changin'. The past century has seen astonishing and radical transformations in just about every aspect of human life. For hundreds, even thousands of years life for the average person changed very little. There were plagues and wars, famines and floods, but the cycle of these events was relatively unvarying. If you lived to maturity and managed to avoid the disasters, then your life would probably be broadly similar to your parents' lives and you would have a pretty good idea of the sort of lives your children would lead.

And so it continued until the machine age. Industrialisation transformed small communities into vast cities with populations dependent on buying rather than growing their own food. Access to education and healthcare soon became widely available. Money values, for centuries much the same, underwent galloping inflation and started to talk in new and seductive ways. Increased mobility shrank the world. Communications systems moved from stagecoach to e-mail and more than 3,500 satellites now orbit the globe.

The speed of change has been accelerating so wildly that today our technology is obsolete before it hits the shops. But there has been a huge price to pay for the lifestyle of the Western World enjoyed by the majority of its citizens. And it cannot be ignored or dismissed as other people's problems. We are living in a world where dangerously lowered immunity to disease, multiple allergies, food safety scares, water shortages, overcrowding and pollution are, in one way or another, affecting us all.

More than ever before, we cannot hold on to a sense of ourselves as unconnected with the whole of life. We are now often painfully aware of our interdependence and the fact that when any aspect of life is in crisis, all aspects of life are in crisis. But it is just this awakened consciousness that is our greatest hope, that can inspire new respect and love of other life forms, global peace initiatives, awareness of human rights, intolerance of cruelty and countless acts of selfless heroism and kindness.

So what part can crystals play in restoring health and balance to our lives?

Crystals have contributed to many key areas of our lives — from building to ceramics, from computers to lasers. But an over-emphasis on the material and technical has brought its own imbalances, and by only using crystals in these ways, we miss completely their sacred uses and healing properties once so respected by our ancient forebears. Throughout the book emphasis will be placed on how crystals have a natural tendency to bring imbalanced energy fields back into balance. I would suggest that by respectfully and consciously working with their sacred energetic properties, we can use crystals to restore much needed harmony in all aspects of our lives.

The purpose of this book is to explore the many practical ways this might be achieved where it matters most — in the inner and outer worlds of ourselves, our homes, our children, our work and our immediate environment. If each of us was to make positive changes within our own spheres, we would change the world!

Crystals can show us many ways of reuniting with our source, honouring our world and walking its pathways with reawakened co-operation, respect and meaning. I hope this book will provide lots of useful ideas and practical ways you can invite crystals to share your life for the benefit of all.

SECTION I

An Introduction to Crystals

Earth's crammed with heaven,
And every common bush afire with God:
But only he who sees takes off his shoes.

Elizabeth Barrett Browning

CHAPTER 1

The Crystal Healing Tradition

The world is charged with the grandeur of God
Gerard Manley Hopkins

L ife was hard in the hunter-gatherer communities of prehistory. While the Ice Age held our planet in its chilling grip, game was scarce and vegetation limited. The difference between starvation and survival could be a single lucky kill or, more likely, a lucky find. The world of these ancient people was bounded by three absolute necessities — food, warmth and shelter. Finding them was a full-time job.

Yet despite the massive pressures of survival, it is a fact that some individuals in virtually every tribe took time to collect crystal. The great mystery is why.

The most obvious explanations will not do. Crystals were not used as currency; archaeologists have not found nearly enough of them at the ancient sites for this to be their function. Nor were they thought of as precious in the way gemstones are today. While some examples of crystal have rarity value — diamonds are an obvious example — these were not the crystal collected. What was looked for was quartz, one of the most common substances on the planet.

Another explanation often put forward was that crystals were picked up for personal adornment, that our distant ancestors simply found them pretty. This won't do either. First of all, there is no evidence of crystals being worn, as jewellery is now worn, to any great degree in tribal communities.

And, more to the point, not all crystal *is* pretty. Quartz can manifest as an unattractive lump of whitish rock.

When I was researching my last book, *Healing with Crystals*,[1] I was fascinated to discover there was a common thread that associated crystals with divine contact — often via angelic messengers — and carrying with them divine powers. Aboriginal and native American stories, ancient Vedic texts, the Old Testament of the Bible, Muslim and rabbinical sources all make reference to crystals as being gifts of the gods. In other words, there has been a widespread belief that crystals are magic.

Special crystals thus became the province of the wise and the powerful, the shaman, the king, the priest, the lama. They were seen as a link between humanity and its divine source, providing the magician with ways of seeing beyond ordinary reality to inner conditions and allowing the king to radiate power and divine authority through his crown. While the stones themselves carried their own power (their unique energetic properties) they were also invested with the energy projections of the people that so revered them, and thus they carried greater and greater meaning and power.

THE SHAMAN'S POWER

There has been a curious similarity in the way crystals have been used in different parts of the world. As far apart as the deserts of Aboriginal Australia, the forests of South America and the jungles of the Malay Peninsula, quartz has for centuries been a stimulant to shamanic prowess.

In each case, crystal fragments are introduced beneath the initiate's skin. For the Cobenos of South America the place for the fragment is the initiate's head, where it is firmly believed to replace his brain and endow him with mystical power. In Australia, powdered crystal, believed to originate in the sky, is inserted beneath the skin of the arms and torso, creating scarring in the form of magical designs. A similar practice is carred out by the Negritos of Malaysia. Interestingly, many of the tribes who engage in these painful practices believe them to be only the second best way of tapping crystal power. The preferred method is for spirit visitors to insert phantom crystals during a dream — an approach that is certainly a great deal easier on the initiate.

SOUL RETRIEVAL

Quartz is also used in Borneo in a curiously impressive ceremony designed to return a lost soul. Certain kinds of mental illness, emotional problems, physical maladies or just plain runs of bad luck are diagnosed as the loss of the soul, which must then be returned to the individual concerned. This is done amidst chants and dancing while the entranced shaman rubs the soulless body with sacred crystal pieces. Aided by the magic of the crystal, the shaman then enters the Netherworld, searches out the wandering soul and leads it back to the person who lost it.

This ceremony, as much as any other, gives the clue to why crystals have always been considered so valuable. For, unlikely though it sounds, the magic works — a point attested to by a great many eyewitness accounts — and the patient gets better. Whether this is actually due to the return of a lost soul is not at issue here. What is at issue is the clear connection between the use of crystals and successful healing.

It is always tempting to attribute the healing to suggestion and dismiss the crystals as window-dressing, but such an approach is superficial since it fails to explain how crystals *became* window-dressing in the first place, in an age when conditions were so harsh that only the most practical techniques were likely to survive. It seems far closer to the mark to postulate that crystals became valued for their indigenous healing properties and that it was these properties which gave them their 'magical' reputation.

Certainly the idea that crystals really do generate a mysterious energy that can influence body and mind is in accord with another extraordinarily widespread example of their use — that of divination.

CRYSTAL GAZING
The crystal ball is a cliché familiar from a hundred fairgrounds and a thousand newspaper cartoons. Yet it is intimately linked with the tradition of crystal healing and has extremely ancient roots.

This is seen in a medicine practice of North America's Cherokee people back into the depths of prehistory. When confronted by illness, the medicine man would typically use quartz crystals for diagnosis as well as cure. They were heated, then laid on the patient's body. The tribal shaman would then squat beside the patient and look into the crystal; or rather, he would look through it, for the technique permitted a sort of depth vision into the body of the patient himself. This may well be a specialist form of induced clairvoyance but, once again, the point is that it works. Diseases are accurately diagnosed. If they were not, the technique would soon be abandoned. If a medicine man loses too many patients, he also loses his prestige, position and livelihood. He has a vested interest in finding effective procedures.

Having made contact with the body of the patient, the crystal was then put in sunlight so that the sun's rays, mystically transformed, could begin a cure. Alternatively, the medicine man might rub crystals vigorously between his hands to energise them before placing them on the patient's body to 'draw out' the pain. Astoundingly, this ages-old technique is virtually identical to the way quartz points and other crystals are used in crystal healing today. The transfer of energy to a highly sensitised Cherokee tribesman could be so strong that he would experience minor convulsions before a cure was effected. While rare in crystal healing today, this phenomenon can still be seen in some of the more emotional forms of 'faith healing' — a misnamed technique that almost certainly involves energy transfer.

From 'looking into' patients as a diagnostic tool, it is a short enough step to using crystals for broader visionary experience. Another Cherokee technique involves placing a piece of quartz into a stream, then watching the pictures that form in the water as it runs over the surface of the stone. Although this may be less due to the energy structures of the crystal than to trance induction by the play of movement, light and shade, it is easy to see how crystals could become associated with visions, and hence predictions. Many thousands of miles from North America, tribal shamans stared fixedly into clear crystal for glimpses of past, present and future. Once again, it is likely that eye fixation on the highly reflective surface of the crystal acted as a trance induction. But in this practice can be clearly seen the forerunner of the crystal ball which, used properly, acts in exactly the same way.

Crystal balls can also produce pictures, although how to interpret them remains a mystery. My husband, open minded but cautious when it comes to unusual phenomena, found that by looking into a clear quartz crystal sphere in the same out-of-focus way that enables you to see those strange 3D laser pictures, produced a startling moving image of an unknown dark-skinned man who turned to look at him from within the crystal. The image disappeared when the strangeness dawned on my husband and he became wildly overexcited. He was able to repeat the experience on another occasion, when he saw the same man walking at a distance.

GEM REMEDIES

But however many visionary or magical techniques were developed, healing has historically remained the prime association with crystals. In the Scottish Highlands, for example, a folk tradition insists on the curative properties of water poured over crystals, then given to cattle. This is a primitive form of what present-day crystal therapists call a 'gem remedy' — a healing approach that traps crystal energies in liquid form — which, along with flower remedies, is referred to as 'vibrational' healing.

In Ireland, crystals have also been used as an aid to health in cattle, but unlike Scotland were most often employed as preventative talismans rather than active cures. Some stones were even believed to rid home and byre of vermin, thus removing the root cause of many diseases. Crystals such as moss agate, which show plant-like patterns just beneath their surface, were used to stimulate crop growth, an example of sympathetic magic that may or may not have been effective, but again links crystals with the idea of nourishment, good health and well-being.

CRYSTALS IN THE BIBLE

The healing tradition of crystals extended out of deep prehistory into biblical times. The patriarch Abraham was credited in the rabbinical tradition with special healing powers because of a magical crystal he wore around his neck. Aaron had a crystal ring which glowed brightly when he — and the nation of Israel — was in the peak of health following an angelic blessing. Whatever the case for angelic influence, there is sound experiential evidence that the light-refracting properties of certain stones do indeed vary with the health of the individual who wears them.

The *Vedas*, India's oldest and most sacred scriptures, link gemstones with astrology and hence with healing, since astrological considerations underlie virtually all forms of Vedic medicine. Through their association with the stars — and it is interesting here to note that several early tribal communities believe crystals to be the gift of the 'star people' — the healing properties of different types of gem are categorised and put to use. As elsewhere, the approach was intensely practical. Dire warnings were issued about the use of inferior quality crystals.

In the early 1940s Dr Benoytosh Bhattacharyya developed a modern system of colour therapy based on the ancient Vedic tradition. It used gem and semi-precious stones to balance the energy spectrum of his patients and thus effect a variety of cures. In the West, modern crystal therapy works in essentially the same way.

CHAPTER 2

The Physical Properties of Crystals

We shall not cease from exploration
And the end of all our exploring
Will be to arrive where we started
And know the place for the first time

T. S. Eliot

Crystals influence just about all areas of our lives. While we inhabit a planet that is largely made up of crystals, we also live in buildings made possible by crystals. Natural stone has a crystalline structure, but so do most artificial building materials, and the cement that binds them depends on crystal growth for it to harden. Without crystals many of the pigments that were used to decorate our shrines and churches would not exist — the rich madonna blue famous in Renaissance painting, for example, relied on ground lapis lazuli for its unique depth. The fresco technique itself involved applying the mineral pigments directly to the wet cement of the wall that, once hardened by crystal activity, made the image an integral part of the structure.

Without crystals we would have no micro computers, modern telecommunications or laser surgery. Crystals and their chemical derivatives also play an important role in orthodox medicine — kunzite, for example, a variety of the crystal group spodumene, is the prime source of lithium, the basis of an important drug used in the treatment of manic depression.

PIEZO-ELECTRICITY

Quartz crystals have been used by shamanic cultures and early civilisations in ceremonies where striking the crystal produced a dramatic flash of light. In my previous book, *Healing with Crystals*, I cite Michael Harner's fascinating account taken from his book, *The Way of the Shaman*, of an experience he had many years ago with the Coast Miwok of California. He observed the 'waking' of a very large quartz crystal. The ceremony involved the shaman of the tribe striking the blunt base of the crystal against a specific rock just off the coast. It was believed by the tribe to be a highly dangerous operation — if the crystal were smashed it would cause the end of the world. When Harner later mentioned having attended this ceremony to a well-known physicist, he was told that the smashing of such a large crystal might well have ended the shaman's world, since the electrical charge it released could easily have killed him.

You can try this (less dangerously) yourself with a small natural quartz point and something as simple as a small mallet to demonstrate one of the fascinating properties of quartz. If you strike the end of a quartz crystal in a darkened room, you will see a brief flash of light at the point. This light is an electrical spark which is produced when the crystal trans-forms *kinetic* energy (the force of the blow) into electrical energy (the spark). Compression of the atoms within the crystal produces electrons and the release of compression allows a minute expansion of the crystal and reabsorption of electrons — and if a very high energy source is applied, the crystal may fracture. The whole process is known as the piezo-electricity (pronounced pie-ee-zo electricity) and this is how most pocket lighters are powered today.

PYRO-ELECTRICITY

Closely associated with piezo-electricity is the *pyro*-electric effect, which describes the effect on crystals produced by variations in temperature, causing an electrified state or polarity. Heat activates the expansion of the crystal's inherent energy and when it cools the energy contracts and is retained within the crystal's structure, sometimes, as in the case of topaz, holding the electrical energy for several hours. To demonstrate this effect, all you need to do is throw the right sort of crystal, such as a tourmaline, into the embers of a small wood or turf fire. As the crystal heats up, it first attracts then suddenly repels the ashes due to a build-up of electrical charges on its surface.

CRYSTAL FREQUENCIES

Scientists experimenting with crystals some years ago began to wonder, as a crystal released a few electrons when you squeezed it and went back to its original shape when you released the pressure (absorbing the missing electrons from the air around it), whether it might be possible to reverse this process. They wondered whether a crystal might actually expand if forced to take in additional electrons and return to normal when the electron stream was switched off.

The idea was easily tested as an electron stream is only an electrical current. So electrodes were attached to a piece of crystal, the power turned on and measurements made. Sure enough, the crystal expanded while the current was on and contracted back to its original size when the current was switched off. Although the movements were tiny — vibrations that cannot be seen with the naked eye — they showed that the really exciting thing about crystal is that when you feed in a measured amount of electricity, the degree of vibration it produces is *absolutely constant*. Any variation is so minute that for all practical purposes it can be discounted.

This utter reliability of the crystal's vibrations made it ideal to be used in radios and television sets, radar installations, computer systems — anywhere that accurate frequency is needed. The watch you are probably wearing right now is a perfect example and its pinpoint accuracy is guaranteed because the little chip of quartz crystal inside it is vibrating to the stimulus of the battery at a totally reliable rate. Clearly then, one of the prime physical characteristics of crystals is that of energy transformation — the energy put into the crystal is not always and not necessarily the same energy that comes out.

LIGHT AND CRYSTAL OPTICS
Shine a white light through a coloured crystal and coloured light comes out. This effect is so commonplace we seldom stop to consider what a miracle it is. In fact, the process is extraordinarily complex. The colour of light is directly related to its wavelength. Impurities in a crystal cause it to absorb certain frequencies of (white) light. Our eyes then pick up only the wavelengths *not* absorbed. The absorbed light gives the crystal its colour. The remaining wavelength determines the precise hue of the light that emerges. You can demonstrate all this simply by hanging a crystal in your window or holding it up to the sun.

A beam of light shone through any crystal (except those belonging to the cubic system) is slowed down and refracted, which means it is bent, and immediately splits into two rays which travel through the crystal at different speeds and are refracted by different amounts. Measuring how far light is bent by a crystal is called the refractive index (RI) and is one way of testing the authenticity of gemstones.

BAR CODES, LASERS AND MISSILES

Every day 2,000 furnaces are fired round the clock to create flame-fusion corundum — synthetically produced ruby and sapphire. Man-made sapphire has even found its way on to supermarket cash-outs. Layered over glass, it virtually eliminates the scratches that can cause the laser to misread the price bar code.

The heart of the first laser was a perfectly pure synthetic crystal rod. The three major qualities of corundum — hardness, high melting point and ability to allow free passage of light waves — form the basis of laser technology. The sapphire is also at the leading edge of silicon chip technology. In high-radiation environments, such as space or nuclear reactors, every now and then a radiation particle penetrates a conventional silicon chip. If it moves through the silicon substrate, the charged particle can upset the chip's operation. But with a sapphire substrate, the whole chip is naturally resistant to stray radiation, as sapphire is an almost perfect insulator.

Sapphires are also at the forefront of weapons technology. A sapphire tube placed near a warplane's engine houses the infra-red countermeasures (IRCM) device programmed to emit very strong signals that match the signals of an enemy craft. This confuses the missile which 'sees' the IRCM carrier as friendly and fails to target it. The latest crystal achievement in missile technology is a missile nose-cone grown from a single crystal — a seamless sphere of transparent sapphire. Sapphire allows the unimpeded passage of optical wavelengths that missile sensors need to lock on to a target, and will not abrade even in a sandstorm.

CRYSTAL PLANET

The remarkable facts about crystals have encouraged broader speculation. One of the most interesting theories was put forward in the 1960s when three Russian scientists suggested planet earth was itself a gigantic crystal. They decided that there was no reason why a latticework pattern — a 'matrix of cosmic energy', as they put it — could not have been built into the earth's structure when it was formed. According to this theory, the earth started life as a crystal and gradually turned into the globe it is today.

The scientists claim the crystal can still be seen as twelve pentagonal slabs covering the earth's surface, a dodecahedron on which are overlaid twenty equilateral triangles. The hypothesis is that the whole geometric structure influenced the sitings of ancient civilisations, due to earth faults and magnetic anomalies on the grid.

While this theory is highly controversial, the idea that the earth has a basic harmonic symmetry is very ancient. It has long been held that certain places on earth are subtly more important than others and that they are very possibly connected. The Russian theory is not very far from the Australian Aboriginal conviction that the well-being of the earth is dependent on keeping its 'crystal web' intact and healthy, an increasingly difficult task in these days of intensive mining, deforestation and chemical pollution.

CHAPTER 3

How to Choose Crystals

Nobody can give you wiser advice than yourself

Cicero

My main interest and work has always involved the quartz group of crystals because of their remarkable energetic and balancing properties. Quartz, more than any other crystal, has an age-old reputation for healing power, and its applications are incredibly diverse. I would therefore suggest that your first experiences with crystals should be with one or more from this large group, the most popular of which includes clear quartz, snowy (white), smoky (brownish black), rose (transluscent pink), amethyst (lavender-violet), citrine (golden yellow), aventurine (green), tiger's eye (gold, brown or blue-grey, sometimes known as hawk's eye) or one of the large range of agates.

It is a good idea to decide, perhaps after reading this book, what use you have in mind for your crystal. Then come the considerations of type, size, shape, quality and cost. Do you want a focusing and personal crystal (a single point) or a cluster, perhaps, for more general influences? Perfect points and clusters are expensive, but they will make wonderful personal crystals or heart stones for the centre of the home or meditation room.

Slightly damaged crystals are fine for home and office use and especially for 'heavy work' such as screening electrical radiation. Damage too can sometimes remind us of the knocks we have inevitably experienced in life and can bring a particularly close affinity with a crystal. There are different schools of thought about the value of working with perfect stones — for example, the Indian ayurvedic tradition prizes perfection highly, whereas the native shaman's most powerful crystals are often extremely worn and battered.

Your choice of crystal will often reflect aspects of your life journey to you. Thus, if you are learning to love and accept your own hurt, you can find great comfort in a crystal that appears to know suffering, but perfect clarity could equally be a gift to the soul. The rainbows that are often found within quartz crystals carry a special gift of hope and joy.

NATURAL QUARTZ POINTS

You will recognise a natural quartz point by its six sided form. These occur in clear, smoky, amethyst (long amethyst points are unusual), citrine and, very rarely, rose quartzes. Commonly, the six sides end in a point (or termination) with six sloping faces leading to the point. Crystal points emit their greatest radiation from this termination channelling their energy from base to tip, whereas an irregular fragment of quartz (such as rough rose quartz — see below) will radiate in all directions, without this focus and concentration.

Because of the directed and focused energy of the natural point, it is very suitable for any purpose which involves the direction of energy, from creating room placements to laying on or around the body for personal energy healing. They are also suitable for channelling and receiving thought and insight in meditation. Double-terminated crystals — that is, with a point at both ends — are sometimes found and these are valuable because of the way energy flows out in both directions.

Stones have an energy radiance in proportion to their mass, so that large stones will be stronger than small stones or, at least, affect a greater area. Exceptions to this rule are when patterns of crystals are set up as 'grids', specifically so that comparatively small stones will 'talk to each other' and influence the energy of a whole room. Because of the way crystals interact, it is important to place your stones with intention — random groups will set up a discordant chatter that does more harm than good.

CLUSTERS AND GEODES

Where several crystals have grown together in clusters or groups, a particularly strong radiating energy results. Large clusters of clear quartz or amethyst, which have the effect of an energy shower, can powerfully affect an entrance or living space. Geodes (formed where crystals have filled a small hollow rock) or small clusters are suitable for intensifying energy in personal healing applications, such as the placing of an apophyllite cluster on the heart centre to enhance awareness and light.

ROUGH STONES

Rough stones are usually those that form massively, that is without any regular *external* geometric form, although their internal atomic structure remains perfect and regular (see Chapter 1). Depending on their size, rough stones such as rose quartz can be used for a wide variety of purposes — to change the energy of a room, to protect your energy field, to balance your sleep patterns or to create gem waters. Straight from the earth, they have a very pure energy and are fine stones to use in healing.

TUMBLED STONES

Tumbled stones are usually made from chips of damaged crystal or from crystals that are 'massive' in structure such as rose quartz. They are tumbled together with water and sand in a mechanical drum which leaves the stones polished and irregular like the pebbles you might find in a riverbed or on the seashore. They are widely available, inexpensive and useful in a variety of ways, especially for children, as tumbling tends to soften and slightly decrease the energetic effect of the stone. When you start working with crystals, tumbled stones are invaluable and are the ideal choice for pocket crystals — every time you handle them, you will be treating your whole body through the reflexology zones on the palm.

PENDANTS, NECKLACES AND JEWELLERY

Wearing a crystal pendant is one of the best ways to affect your energy field positively, provided you make sure you cleanse your crystal regularly, enabling it to continue its work of tranformation without becoming tired or gummed up. Any form of pendant will work well, using the crystal of your choice (for the attributes of individual stones, see Section VI: the Colour Crystal Directory) and it does not harm the energy of the crystal for it to be mounted in silver or gold. Metal alloys are less desirable because they often irritate the skin.

A full necklace made of stones will have a more intense effect than a single pendant, with round beads being the gentlest and faceted stones the strongest. Among the lovely examples available you will easily find amethyst, clear quartz, blue lace agate, aventurine, jade, citrine and garnet. They will bring the strong protection and qualities of their individual natures.

Special jewellery in the form of a ring (often a token of love and fidelity), ear-rings, necklaces or brooches can have a powerful effect according to the cutting and setting of the stones. The energy of the stone is usually most effective when in direct contact with the skin, so an open-backed setting is a good idea. If you are looking for a piece of jewellery with real power, such as a talisman, it is best to look for a craftsman who creates individual pieces that have been dictated by the stone, rather than the mass-produced standard items most common in the high street.

THE EFFECTS OF FORM

Specially cut crystals — those where changes have been imposed on the crystal's natural form — will work according to the shape imposed. Spheres are very popular because the form reflects an all-round, all-encompassing radiance. This is usually beneficial, but the crystal's direction of growth and structure will also remain held within the created form. If you attempt a meditation (see Chapter 17, pp 180) to enter a crystal sphere you may find the lack of gravity disorientating, but it is a good way to experience the type of energy you are working with.

Any geometry deliberately superimposed on a crystal will give a particular focus, but it is essential that the crystal be cut sympathetically. The gem cutter knows that incorrect cutting can kill the fire and irreparably damage a valuable stone. There are many crystal prisms on the market nowadays. These are natural quartz points that have been hand polished along their natural sides and facets and usually sit on a flat base. If well done, the energy of the crystal is considerably amplified and its radiance enhanced. However, the mind of the polisher has become involved with the crystal, so sympathy and consciousness are vital. Use your own sensitivity to tune in to this.

A well-cut pyramid form might be a good choice for the central focus of a meditation room or group, the structure holding a particularly concentrated and balanced geometry that will influence the mind and the energy field in a room. A crystal wand that has been knowledgeably polished along the crystal's natural geometry can also greatly strengthen the effect of the crystal. However, my first crystals of choice will always remain those in their natural form, whether massive lumps, as in rough rose quartz, quartz points or amethyst beds. Natural crystals can be used in almost all the applications described in this book.

CHOOSE WITH YOUR HEART

You will find some books that give intricate details about the exact form of individual crystals — the number of sides to the faces, triangular and diamond formations etc. While these can be significant and even important when you have some experience with crystals, it is a good idea to start out free of such intellectual categories which can interrupt the flow of energy between the crystal and your heart. Call me a romantic, but I like to choose my crystals like my friends — with my heart first, and afterwards allow the head its say. Centre yourself, slow your breathing and scan the crystals until you find one that especially draws or calls to you. You will know it when you find it.

As with your close friends, you will discover the unique beauty of your crystal, loving the faults or damage as much as the pristine perfection. Spend a few moments examining the crystal in the light. Marvel at the beautiful facets of light, rainbows, whole galaxies contained within your crystal. Then *close your eyes* and form a link with your crystal.

EXERCISE YOUR INTUITION

As intuition is an invaluable asset to those who wish to bring crystals into their lives, I suggest you try out ways of exercising your intuitive faculty. Pendulums are a marvellous intuitive tool. They can be used for dowsing, in diagnosis and for prescribing remedies, for energy balancing, as well as a multitude of other purposes. A pendulum that is made from a natural quartz point (or any other natural crystal) carries the energetic properties of the crystal which will influence its function as a pendulum. For regular dowsing it is best to use an ordinary pendulum (made from wood or resin), especially if you are just starting to develop your dowsing skills.

Pendulum Exercise

Centre yourself, spine straight, shoulders relaxed and breathing deeply from the belly. Hold the pendulum lightly from the top of its cord or chain. Relax and *tell yourself* that the pendulum will begin to turn clockwise. Wait and do not consciously move your hand, but just allow your unconscious to contact you through the pendulum. It will seem to move on its own, but actually your hand moves it involuntarily in co-ordination with your unconscious mind. If it does not move, deliberately start it off to get the feel of what you want. Then stop and wait again for it to occur without your conscious interference. I suggest you use a clockwise direction for yes or positive (+) and anticlockwise for no or negative (-).

Once you have established firm indications for both directions, you can 'test' your intuitive skills. A simple exercise involves using several, identical, plain boxes or envelopes, one of which conceals an object (or sheet of paper). Mix them up, then use your pendulum to 'find' the hidden object. As with most underused faculties, your ability will improve with practice, and eventually you may develop your own distinctive dowsing language for

detecting a variety of things such as water or the presence
of certain chemicals.

Chapter 4

Caring for your Crystals

Cleanliness is next to godliness

Traditional

Life in its simplest and most primitive manifestation is sometimes defined in terms of growth and reaction to stimuli. By applying just these two criteria it's possible to conclude that a rabbit is a living organism, while a brick is not. Given time enough and food, little bunnies grow into big bunnies and, little or big, they'll both hop away if you poke them gently with a stick. A brick, on the other hand, just sits there however long you leave it or however much you poke it.

But when you apply this standard life test to crystals, a very unexpected result emerges. The first thing you notice is that they satisfy the first part of the definition. Unlike any other (supposedly) inert substance, crystals have a tendency to grow. Some types grow slowly, on a time-scale of hundreds, thousands, sometimes even millions of years. Others, like sugar crystals in a saturated solution, grow so quickly you can actually see them forming. But all crystal lattices in their natural form will grow in a suitable environment, just like a rabbit.

Of course, no crystal reacts if you poke it with a stick — unless, that is, you poke it very hard. If the crystal is a member of the quartz family, striking it sufficiently sharply *will* result in a reaction: it will generate a spark. That's a different reaction to that of the rabbit, but it is a reaction none the less and one that appears predictably and repeatedly. Quartz crystals, it seems, no more like being poked than do bunnies.

It is eerie to realise crystals are capable of passing one of the standard scientific tests for life forms. We reject the finding almost instinctively. A crystal is just a piece of rock. It can't be alive. It doesn't move. At least the rabbit runs away. Yet with a few rare exceptions like the American tumbleweed, trees and plants don't run away either, and we have no problem at all accepting them as living.

However lightly I've talked of bricks and bunnies, this is not a whimsical investigation of crystalline life potential. Sober scientists studying the behaviour patterns of crystals have been forced (reluctantly) to the conclusion that these structures represent at the very least an interim step between inert matter and living tissue. No scientist has yet been prepared to risk his reputation by announcing categorically that crystals are alive. But every honest scientist will admit they aren't dead either.

So, even at our most cautious, we have to admit that with crystals we *might* be dealing with living systems.

THE IMPORTANCE OF RELATIONSHIP

This finding has important implications for any of you who have decided you want to bring crystals into your life and work with them. For you can no more expect crystals to thrive on neglect than you would a puppy or a kitten. This is not a fanciful comparison. We have all, unfortunately, seen the listless eyes and poor condition manifested by ill-treated pets. Amazingly, ill-treated crystals will show very similar symptoms. Although it can take some time, they will eventually lose their sparkle and even their colour. Their ability to generate and transform energy will gradually diminish. Eventually they will turn into dull, listless, lifeless lumps of rock.

Happily, the converse is equally true. When crystals are well cared for, they retain — or even enhance — their clarity and colour and become energised to a degree that is virtually palpable. Although it runs contrary to every scientific theory I have ever heard, my personal experience — and that of several colleagues — has been that well cared-for quartz crystals used regularly for meditation purposes will lose any initial cloudiness and become progressively more transparent (another form of reaction to a stimulus that suggests a living being).

From experience I have come to the opinion that the power and efficacy of crystals is directly affected by the quality of your relationship with them — to the extent that the crystal may be seen as 'sleeping' in its natural state and 'awakened' to greater potential by its relation to the human and, just as importantly, human potential can be awakened and developed by contact with crystals.

So how do you take good care of your crystals? If you begin with the idea that you are dealing with living creatures, a great deal of what follows will sound no more than common sense. You don't need to feed them, like your family or pets, but just like them they need sunshine, fresh air, clean water, regular grooming, 'exercise' and, most of all, attention and affection.

THE ENVIRONMENT

For crystals that you use in your home, let them spend as much time as possible on a sunny dust-free window sill, with occasional holidays in your garden or window-box. Don't worry about leaving them out in the rain — most crystals love it (except for water-soluble crystals which I'll deal with later). They also love direct sunlight and moonlight.

For crystals you wear in the form of pendants, necklaces etc., try to make sure they get as much light as possible. In other words, wear them proudly outside your clothes. If you have been advised to wear a particular crystal next to your skin for therapeutic purposes, make sure to give it time off and rinse your pendant in running water each day to discharge the static which builds up. What I've just said about holidays for house crystals applies to crystals which are worn as well.

Next, keep your crystals clean, clearing them of any energy/information build-up. For quartz, at least once a fortnight — more often if it looks dull and depleted — soak your crystal in a solution of 2 tablespoons of sea salt to 2 pints of spring water for a minimum of an hour. (You can leave it up to six hours if it's very tired, especially if you've just bought it and don't know how it's been treated.)

As an alternative, you can collect rain water in a clear glass or natural container (a wooden barrel is ideal) and use that to bathe your crystals, omitting the salt. Sea water is another excellent cleansing medium and your crystals will love the Neptunian energy it brings. Sacred well or spring water will bring the special blessing of the site from which the water comes. This is an especially good treatment for healing crystals.

Because of the harsh effects of salt in contact with some crystals, but because of its powerful energetic clearing properties, Michael Gienger, in *Crystal Power, Crystal Healing*, recommends laying your crystal in a clear glass dish which has been embedded in a larger salt-filled dish. In this way delicate stones will not suffer.

CHARGING WITH SUN AND MOONLIGHT

When the soaking period is over, rinse the crystal in clear spring water and pat it dry with a soft white cotton cloth.

Then leave it for at least four hours in direct light, preferably outside on the earth. Early morning and early evening sunlight is ideal as high noonday sun will have a discharging effect on the crystal. Full moonlight also works well and using both sun and moonlight will balance the masculine and feminine energies.

If you use crystals for healing, they should be quick-cleansed after each session by running them under a cold tap, point downwards. Healing is heavy duty work for crystals and they tend to pick up and transform negative (disease) influences from patients. So never, never miss out on their cleaning. You're simply asking for trouble if you do.

Meditation crystals you use yourself don't need such frequent cleaning, as your own energy blends with the crystal's energy and tends to keep you both in good condition. But if you lend out your meditation crystal or use it for frequent energy boosts, make sure it gets recharged in sunlight and/or salt water regularly.

DELICATE CRYSTALS
There are certain crystals that cannot be cleansed using any of the methods I have already given. Halite is a classic example — it's a salt and therefore water soluble. If you bathe it as described above, it will simply vanish!

Other stones that are damaged in water include:

calcites	bornite	apophyllite
gypsums	selenite	celestite
halites (salts)	talc	azurite.

Citrine (very often artificially heat-treated amethyst) may be fragile.

Don't use detergents on:
fluorite, azurite, malachite or chrysocolla.

Never use salt on:
opal, apophyllite or celestite.

For all of the above, you must use one or other of the following alternative cleansing methods.

SMUDGING

Smudging is a traditional Native American technique which involves burning a mixture of desert sage, sweet grass and cedar, all of which are available from New Age shops and (some) health stores either individually or in the form of smudge sticks. Smudge outdoors if possible, or at least well away from anything that might be damaged by sparks.

For the process, you'll need a large shell (abalone is traditional) or heat-proof bowl, a fan or feathers and matches.

Place the loose herbs or smudge stick in the shell or bowl and light them. When the surface is burning well, blow out the flame, leaving the herbs smouldering and smoking. Firstly smudge yourself by drawing the smoke with cupped hand to your heart, over your head, down your arms and down the front and back of your body to the ground. Traditionally you then offer the smoke to the six directions: upwards to Spirit, down to Mother Earth, then to the north, east, south and west. Although this is the order of the native American tradition, you may be more familiar with starting in the east through south, west and north, then below and finishing above. Use the sequence you are most comfortable with, but always move clockwise with the sun. After the offering you can smudge each of your crystals individually, consecrating them with the smoke. You can also smudge the room you are working in, paying special attention to the corners, doors and windows. (Incense can be used in a similar way, incidentally, but you need to select an incense with specific cleansing properties.)

AMETHYST BED

A lovely gentle way of clearing your crystals (especially useful for healers) is to place them on a bed of amethyst druse — a large cluster of amethyst crystals — as the iron atoms in the amethyst, in combination with the quartz, will ensure a powerful clearing of stored material. They will need a minimum of one hour, if not over-tired, but a full twenty-four hours is recommended. It is quite safe to leave crystals to rest on amethyst whenever they are not being used.

BREATH CLEANSING

Cleansing with the breath is a very effective technique which both charges and cleans, but is suitable only for crystal points and tumbled stones, not lattices. I first came across it in *The Newcastle Guide to Healing with Crystals* by Pamela Chase and Jonathan Pawlik, tried it and found it worked extremely well. Hold the crystal, point upwards, with your index finger on the largest facet and inhale deeply. Hold your breath briefly while visualising the crystal clearing. Continue this visualisation while you exhale slowly through your nostrils on to the crystal. Do this several times until the crystal feels clean. If you think it necessary, you can also visualise a fountain of light flowing from the base to the point and flowing all round the crystal, then working from the centre out to the sides.

HEALING OF THE EARTH

Sometimes your crystals will need more than cleaning. If a crystal has been severely neglected or overworked, it will actually require healing. By far the best way to do this is to bury the crystal in soil and let it receive the comfort of Mother Earth. Leave a little piece showing so you can find it again. If you bury small stones, mark the spot well or bury them in a clay pot with the rim left showing. Turn and check it occasionally until you find it has regained colour and vitality. This process can take anything up to six months. In exceptional cases you may find it necessary to leave a stone in the ground indefinitely.

When travelling, wrap your crystals in soft, white, *natural*-fibred cloth such as silk, linen or cotton. Shamans carry their crystals in hide medicine bags or in little thonged leather pouches around their necks. Personal crystals should not be passed around or displayed publicly if you want them to hold their charge.

When crystals are not treated gently, the results can be unfortunate. Clean and store stones of varying hardness separately, as the soft ones will be damaged by contact with harder ones. Crystals such as celestite, calcite and apophyllite are among those that crumble very easily.

DEDICATION AND CHARGING

Finally, it's important to dedicate your working crystals. Here intention is vital. Suggest to yourself that the crystal works 'with love and light for the highest good of all whom it contacts'. Alternatively, you can ask for special help in healing, use a prayer of dedication or blessing, or visualise a symbol of balance and unity such as the cross within the circle, the sun or a radiant six pointed star. Once again using the breath and holding the crystal as described above, inhale, hold your breath and visualise it becoming charged with light, vitality and love. Energy follows thought, so you will sense and even see an effect. Continue while you exhale in short bursts through your nose on to the crystal. Repeat several times until the job is done.

The shamanic traditions emphasise the use of the elements in charging crystals and there is no doubt that crystals are empowered by being placed on the earth (some traditions suggest in a high place) to be charged by the light of the sun and the moon, especially at powerful times — when the moon is full or new and at the summer or winter solstice.

CHAPTER 5

How Crystals can Improve your Life

*As a precious stone appeareth a prize in the eyes of him
that obtaineth it;
withersoever it turneth it prospereth*

Proverbs 17:8

While everybody has complained about the weather for
centuries, it's only recently that anybody has made a
serious attempt to do anything about it. The problem
has been that weather is what scientists call a 'chaotic
system'. This means, essentially, that it has so many variables
you can never really work out what it's going to do next.

The chaotic nature of weather may come as a surprise to
those of us accustomed to listening to the forecast in the
morning and finding, by and large, it's usually right. Certainly
weather forecasting techniques have improved in the last
three decades, mainly due to satellite technology. But there's
a wealth of difference between spotting a cold front (rain)
just before it hits the country and accurately forecasting what
the weather will be doing this time next year. Theoretically
that next-year forecast should be possible — you simply
devise a formula that lets you calculate all the variables. But
in a chaotic system like weather, the variables are just *too
numerous*.

But help is at hand. In 1975 the experts started using
fractal geometry.

Fractals are geometric figures featuring something called
self-similarity. What that means is that if you examine any

area of the figure, you'll find it is a smaller copy of the larger portion. It doesn't sound exciting, but when you plot fractals on a computer you create designs of outstanding interest and beauty. Not only that, they look *right* — and for a very interesting reason. It's now known that nature itself follows the rules of fractal mathematics in creating physical terrain.

The discovery has led to something that is exciting scientists enormously — the development of Chaos Theory. Fractal mathematics, with its principle of self-similarity, has given us our first real handle on chaotic systems like the weather, or our global environment as a whole. It allows us to discover patterns in what has always appeared to be chaos. It seems that chaos has an underlying order after all.

Although Chaos Theory is still in its very early days, it has already given us one quite astonishing insight into the nature of reality. Admittedly it's an insight mystics have tried to pass on for generations, except that most of us weren't listening. It's the insight that everything, but everything, is absolutely and intimately connected.

In a picturesque example of this insight, Chaos Theory assures us that the quivering of a butterfly's wings in the Amazon forest can cause a typhoon over China. This is not presented as a fanciful analogy or mythic truth. It is seen by scientists as literal reality.

The implications of the 'butterfly effect' are dramatic. It means you can no longer reasonably see yourself as something apart from the rest of the world. Every action you take, every thought you think, has an influence on the world around you. One wrong step and you too might trigger a typhoon over China.

While much of this book is concerned with ways crystals might improve your environment, it no longer makes sense to treat outer reality as if it was somehow different from yourself. Action follows thought and action, as we have seen, has implications for the entire world. Thus your thoughts carry an influence that extends far beyond the confines of your head.

Even without the insights of Chaos Theory, a little thought will quickly convince you that your external reality is very much a reflection of your inner world. Even if I have never met you before, I can tell a great deal about the sort of person you are by examining the way you dress, the sort of house you live in and the district in which that house is located. Your clothes, the colours you select to paint your walls, the type of furniture you favour all indicate values and preferences that start in your mind.

Admittedly your direct influence over your environment becomes less obvious as the distance increases. It's easy to see that while you have a great deal of control over the way you dress and decorate your home, the shaping of your community or country may only be obvious to you in far smaller ways — a note in the electoral register, perhaps, or a statistic in some government file.

But remember the butterfly effect. The obvious signs are a far cry from the whole story. You may think of yourself as a drop in the ocean, but the largest ocean is still made up of no more than single drops, and even a tiny change in its temperature will influence the ecology of the whole planet.

So if you elect to make changes to your life, the ripple effect can be very far reaching indeed. It's a scary thought. We can no longer pass the buck or shift the blame for any part of life we don't happen to like very much because we're indivisibly right in the middle of the whole shebang. It can also seem a heavy responsibility, but maybe it doesn't have to be so much a burden as a dance — a wonderful, extraordinary, playful celebration of life and all its potential — of being and becoming.

And in that being and becoming, crystals can be an enormous help.

REBALANCING OURSELVES AND OUR ENVIRONMENT

Never in recorded history has humanity been subject to so many stresses. The price we have paid for our complex and prosperous Western lifestyle is high indeed as our depressed immunity and superbug viruses bear witness. It is increasingly difficult to be sure of the safety of the food we eat, the drugs we take, the water we drink and even the air we breathe. As I have stated already, crystals have a tendency to return energy fields to balance. This is applicable both to ourselves and to our environment and crystals can be used in practical ways to counter some of the more negative effects that are an inevitable part of modern living.

POWER SOCKET AND ELECTRICAL FIELD RADIATION

While most of us depend on, and are glad of the benefits of electricity, electrical radiation can come from overhead power cables, domestic appliances and power sockets, and this may contribute to a variety of illnesses, especially in those who are already vulnerable — the elderly, the young or those already run down or weakened by ill health. Geopathic stress — a natural form of radiation usually generated by underground watercourses — is another different but associated problem that may also contribute to ill health. This energy can carry up through the house and can be troublesome, particularly in areas directly over the geopathic 'wave'. Possible ill effects of geopathic stress may actually be made worse because it is also believed to enter the house via the electrical circuitry, as well as being carried by cables, substations and pylons — not a comforting thought as it can affect our homes and workplaces through appliances like storage heaters, computers, microwave ovens and electric blankets.

Dr Mike Adams published his article, 'Crystal Antidotes to Power-Socket Radiation', in *Leading Edge* (Spring 1991), describing his research into the weakening effects of radiation leaking from ordinary 13 amp sockets while looking into the possible causes of his wife's illness. He suggests that, not only can power socket radiation be picked up directly through the top of the head, from the brow upwards, but that it can be carried in our food and drink. He concludes that the combined effects of direct and 'consumed' radiation could be responsible for fatigue, insomnia and contributing factors to illnesses such as MS, ME and some cancers. Whether or not you believe radiation to be a serious risk, blocking off the source of the leakage is a sensible preventative measure and Dr Adams discovered that quartz crystals were the most effective tool for the job.

SIMPLE COMPASS TEST
You can test for electrical radiation leakages with an ordinary compass. Align your compass so that the needle faces north, and move it towards the appliance or power socket steadily. Electromagnetic disturbance will make the compass needle fluctuate. Testing this technique some years ago on our electric blanket, I was horrified to see the compass needle oscillate wildly over the bed, despite the fact that the blanket was switched off. While radiation is greatly reduced by pulling the plug out at the socket, as well as switching off

after using an appliance, the placement of a quartz cluster under the bed completely cleared the field set up by the electric blanket.

If you detect a problem at the socket itself, then this is where you should place the crystal. I keep a quartz cluster on top of the TV set and another between me and my computer monitor. Check any appliances that get regular or prolonged use.

TREATING AT SOURCE

Crystals from the quartz group (clear, smoky, rose, amethyst, citrine etc.) should be used to deal with radiation and they may even be able to stop it from entering the house cables altogether. Try placing a large crystal (7-10 cm wide and about 4 cm across) or cluster to the side or on top of the main fuse box, with the main point or points facing away or laid lengthways, parallel to the wall. The exact placement of the crystals can be determined by checking with your compass until you get a steady reading. Check your appliances after treating the fuse box and you may find you won't need to treat them individually at all. I'm not sure what determines whether or not the fuse box treatment is fully successful. It may simply depend on the quantity of electricity being used, or the size of the crystal.

Crystals used for this type of heavy duty work should be cleansed regularly and thoroughly — at least once a month — and it is preferable to keep two crystals for this purpose, so that they can work in rotation — one month on, followed by a month's well-earned holiday.

Wearing a small natural quartz point as a pendant will give you permanent protection if you cleanse it daily. Take Bach Flowers Rescue Remedy if you find you suffer a worsening of symptoms or a slightly unpleasant flu-like withdrawal for a few days after setting up the crystal protections. Dr Adams makes the point that we have all adapted to receiving this radiation and so we will also need to adapt to the cleaner energy field.

GEOPATHIC STRESS

Traditionally, geopathic stress is tackled by dowsing the house and the immediate environment to establish the location of any trouble spots and the direction and flow of the stress. Copper rods (copper piping cut to the length of the dowsed stress wave) are then buried in the ground outside at the point of entry in order to interrupt the flow. While very effective, this method is not practicable for many living in flats or in urban environments, where there is paving, concrete or asphalt outside. Setting up a crystal grid is an easy solution.

Crystal grids — the placement of a particular number of crystals of an equal size in a geometric pattern — create a clear, balanced energy field and can be used in any situation where pristine space is desirable. Through their interaction (the crystals 'talk' to each other) a contained field is created which transforms any imbalances or disturbance.

CROSS-QUARTER GRID

A cross-quartered grid of four crystals can be used not only to earth geopathic stress, but to create a general-purpose sacred space. For one room, you will need four equal-sized clear quartz points, each about 5–10 cm in length. Place one crystal point into each of the four corners of the room, pointing towards the centre, so that if you join up the points with imaginary lines you create a large X, the lines bisecting at the centre. For a softer energy, try using four equal-sized pieces of rose quartz.

Not only is this very easily made, it is also portable, so you can use it to create a clear hotel room, a temporary healing or seminar space or to keep the energies of the home and work space well balanced and harmonious. Using proportionally larger crystals, you could create a grid outside that contains the whole house and even the garden. Perhaps ancient sacred sites such as Stonehenge and Avebury grid our landscape in a similar way.

Some of the following information on sacred numbers and crystal grids was covered in my previous book *Healing with Crystals* but, as it is so fundamental and useful to so many crystal applications, it bears repetition.

CRYSTAL GRIDS AND THE POWER OF NUMBERS

There is an inherent vibration and proportion in different geometries, so that a grid of four crystals will have a different effect to that made of six or seven. This use of sacred geometry is beneficial in a variety of ways. Try the six pointed Star of David grid (described below) for a particularly good healing energy around a person's photograph. Make it from tumblestones or tiny quartz points, and you will positively affect the owner. Astrologers might note the effects if setting up a healing grid around a birth chart to help offset any difficult aspects. This concept is somewhat alien to our usual material thinking, but I know it to be very effective. If this vibrational approach appeals to you, do experiment and record your results to get a better understanding of what can be done.

One is the number of the individual, independence and, potentially, individuation — Jung's term for the conscious integration of all accessible aspects of the self. Not strictly a grid, one is the number of the power-generating centre. One crystal will radiate energy with an outgoing, spreading effect. A large single crystal at the centre of a circle of people will unify the energy of the group and can be a central focus for group meditation.

When another is added to one, polarity and relationship are created. **Two** balances polarities such as top and bottom, front and back, opposite sides, male and female, inner and outer, *yin* and *yang*, light and dark. It sets up an energy that bounces between the two poles and harmonises energy. The classic symbol of the Tao expresses this dance of energy most elegantly.

Tao symbol

You can work with two crystals in all sorts of ways. In Chapter 7 you will find simple instructions for balancing your personal energy with two crystals. By using a compass to determine true north, you can place one crystal in the north and another in the south to align a room's energies to the energy poles of the earth — this is especially helpful in a bedroom as it encourages peaceful sleep. Another layout that will create a harmonious space for relaxation and healing is to place a quartz point (point towards you) or cluster on the floor at the front and back of your chair or at the top and bottom of your bed.

CREATIVITY

The number **three** is associated with creative self-expression and the joy of living. The sacred trinity symbolises the union of spirit, energy and matter, which combine to create manifestation. This is dynamic, energetic life! Matthew Goodwin describes three as that through which the artist finds expression — writing, painting, sculpting, singing, composing— and it is also through three that we express our feelings for others. This number has a lovely energy of enthusiasm and optimism. A grid of three is excellent for the artist's studio or writer's study and for generating an awareness of life's abundance and joy.

To enhance creativity, place two crystals at the base of a triangle pointing towards the apex of the triangle, with a crystal at the apex of the triangle with its point *inwards* to bring creative *inspiration*, or with its point *outwards* to assist creative *expression*. The exact positioning of this creative trine grid will depend on the form your creativity takes. For example, in a studio the grid may be placed so that the apex of the triangle is close to the artist wishing to be inspired, or to the canvas which is the point of expression.

Four is associated with the square which is the symbol for earth. Its energy is grounded, containing, well ordered and well earthed. This energy is particularly useful for earth-related matters or when you need to have your feet on the ground. It is also associated with limitation in the service of others. The most common of the grids of four is the cross-quartered grid described above for combating geopathic stress, but there is a variation incorporating the four directions. This will balance the elemental influences according to the cardinal points of the compass and is the basis of the grid used in the medicine wheel (see Chapter 15, page 156). Discover the exact compass alignments of the room or space you wish to influence and place a crystal at east, south, west and north, pointed tips facing towards the centre.

The **five** pointed star, the pentagram, is associated with the five elements (earth, water, fire, air and ether or spirit). The balancing of these five elements is central to Western esoteric thought and occurs in many other traditions, notably Ayurveda. The lesson of five is not to dissipate energy and potential but to balance the elements to bring about expansion and limitless potential.

The finest use of five for an environmental grid is to place spirit at the centre of a square grid of four. In other words, place your crystals as suggested above in the cross-quartered or four directions layout and place a fifth crystal at the centre of the grid to symbolise the energy of spirit. If it is possible to hang the crystal, point downwards, at the centre of a room, you will feel both the balance of four and the sacred potential of five. If you cannot hang the crystal, place a crystal, point upwards, on the floor or on a table at the centre. You will notice the energy is slightly different in each case. To use the geometry for five for group work, you could try a pentagram ray by placing five quartz points in the centre of the room, on the floor or on a table, points directed outwards in a five pointed star formation.

THE SIX POINTED STAR

Six finds its most perfect balance in the form of the six pointed star, the Star of David. This star is formed from the double triangle which symbolises the union and balancing of spirit inspiring matter (the downward pointing triangle) and matter aspiring to spirit (the upward pointing triangle). One triangle pushes upwards, reaching to spirit from an earthed base; the other triangle pushes downwards from spirit and pierces matter. It is also the beautifully realised synthesis of the masculine and feminine principles. This star form is one of the finest energies you can work with in healing and spiritual work.

The Star of David grid is the supreme personal balancer. You can create the grid around a chair or on the floor or mattress for a grid you can lie within. Take six cleansed single terminated quartz points. Place each one on the floor about 50 cm from the body, pointing inwards, one behind the chair or about 50 cm from the body at centre, one in front of the chair about 50 cm in front of the feet (or below the feet if lying down), one aligned with each shoulder and one aligned with each knee. Lying down creates an elongated star but it is equally effective. You could also create a six pointed ray, good for a meditation group, by placing the six quartz points in the centre of the room, on the floor or on a table, points outwards in the star formation, to create a beautiful atmosphere of harmony and peace.

Seven is an introspective number and grids of seven are good for self-analysis, self-knowledge and all inner work.

Concerned with spiritual rather than material realities and values, seven encourages deep study and meditation. The seven rayed star grid sets seven crystals, points inwards, evenly around the sacred enclosure. It will bring an energy of high mental attunement and encourage deep understanding and insight.

The number **eight**, as double four, teaches about material reality and the lessons of functioning in, and understanding the energy of, the material world. Eight requires awareness of limitations and has rather a heavy energetic quality, but tackling personal limitations is vital if true mastery is to be accomplished. The best grid to bring you right up against self-limitation and restriction is the double square mandala. It is useful when you wish to work with these energies to bring greater understanding. Any somewhat claustrophobic effects can bring useful insights, but don't expect it to be particularly soothing or comfortable. Place the crystals, points inwards, at each corner and then halfway between each corner, creating a second square set diagonally within the first.

Nine is a really magical number and the flipside of one. It is about the power of giving away power. St Francis reminds us that 'it is in giving that we receive'. Service to humanity is paramount to the individual working with the power of nine, either directly serving others or through giving of the self in creative expression. Nine is associated with the deep mysteries of Self in relation to the All, microcosm and macrocosm. This energy spirals inwards to the centre and then returns outwards in constant dance or double helix. Spiralling energy is more 'feminine' and intuitive than 'masculine' and constructive. The nine sisters at the cauldron of Cerridwen, the nine Muses and, in Arthurian legend, the nine sisters on the Isle of Avalon, give us some sense of the archetypal significance and mysterious power spun and unravelled by nine.

An outdoor spiral grid layout of nine crystals is described in detail in Chapter 15. To walk the spiral is a moving mystery, taking you on a journey to the deep centre and returning you back out through the spiral into the world, transformed. A meditation to accompany this spiral walk is given in Chapter 19.

Crystals in the Home

Bless this house and all who in her dwell
May we prosper and love each other well.
May shining crystals help us light our ways,
Soothe our nights and brighten all our days.

House blessing

Your home is very much an extension of yourself and as such plays a vital part in your health and well-being. While healing affects all aspects of your life, you will find a chapter on Crystal Healing in this section, as the techniques described are central to a healthy home. Moving house is one of the top ten stressers in life, right up there with birth, marriage and bereavement, so it is worth enlisting all the support you can in establishing a harmonious and happy home. The popularity of *feng shui* has made many of us more conscious of the importance of balancing different aspects in our living space and offers a practical system of cures for common problems, always with a view to harmonising the elements and increasing the beneficial flow of *ch'i* (life force energy). This section explores ways crystals can be used, either as part of *feng shui*, or in their own right, to create healthy and harmonious spaces that will feel warm and welcoming, while dispelling disruptive or harmful influences.

Whether you view them as spiritual acknowledgments or having a purely psychological benefit, house blessings and associated rituals can be very helpful, especially when you move into a new home and at times of special change, easing the transition for all concerned. I have included suggestions in the following chapters which you could adapt or which might encourage you to create your own, as well as meditation and self-help exercises where relevant. Please read through the exercises carefully before using them.

CHAPTER 6

Crystal Healing

*The human soul needs beauty even more than
it needs bread*

D.H. Lawrence

It is my belief that healing is a process that takes place
when conditions are right for the individual to let go of
disease. Because we are accustomed to treating ourselves
rather like a car that just goes until it breaks down, we don't
consider the possibility that symptoms we manifest are valid
forms of self-expression at particular points in our lives. It is
a fact that common ailments such as colds and flu increase
dramatically if we are not happy with some aspect of our life
or work. While a virus may go the rounds, you won't pick it
up unless it will serve you in some way — maybe enabling
you to stay home from problems at work or to justify an
overdue rest from a demanding family — or unless your
immune system is already depressed, possibly for the same
reason. If we are subjected to inharmonious circumstances
and attitudes such as harsh living conditions, destructive
relationships, self-hatred, despondency and despair, this will
ultimately show up in the physical body. Equally, loving
kindness and attitudes that reflect that back into the world
can work miracles.

For healing to take place, you need to be as clear as possible. For some it is necessary, or at least helpful, to understand
their own process; for others it is enough to open themselves
up to the willing possibility of change. Crystals can help to

bring about conditions conducive to healing which essentially help to restore your energy field and your environment to a natural balance. To that extent at least, I would suggest that healing is an integral part of your everyday life.

CLEANLINESS

To work with and benefit from healing conditions it is as important to keep yourself clean and clear as it is to cleanse and look after your crystals. Maintain the highest possible standards of personal hygiene as dirt attracts and holds negative energies such as fear, anger and pain. If you are treating others, it is a good idea to keep special clothes for your healing work.

PROTECTION

Don't attempt healing practices when you are out of sorts, as you risk stealing energy from those you wish to help. At these times, and as a natural part of your life, you should pay attention to your own needs. Give yourself the healing space and quiet time you need and invite the appropriate crystal to help you restore your energy balance. Most healers are naturally empathetic and have auras that can absorb everything like a sponge. Great spiritual adepts can learn how to absorb and *transform* negative energies within themselves, but without safeguards most of us lesser mortals merely absorb the disturbed energy that is released in healing and wonder why we feel tired and out of sorts afterwards.

To avoid taking on the other person's pain or distress, protect yourself by carrying or wearing a clean crystal that you have specifically asked to help you keep clear. You can also smudge yourself with sweet grass, sage and other herbs, according to the native American tradition (see page 29) or devise a ritual for yourself. The simple ritual below is an example of how to stay mindful not to absorb the negative conditions you are helping to release.

A Cleansing Ritual

Before you give healing, wash your hands in cool water and call on the protection of the Holy Spirit and of your angels and guardians. Imagine yourself surrounded by violet light and feel the connection of energy through your head and feet, your heart and hands as you say:

I call on the protection of the Holy Spirit, my Angels and Guardians. Bathe me and seal me in the strong protection of your violet flame that I may do your work in safety.

When you have finished your work, wash your hands again carefully and once more imagine yourself bathed in violet light, saying:

As I bathe my hands I call on the power of the Holy Spirit, my Angels and Guardians ... to cleanse me ... and to transform the sickness I have touched ... into wholeness and beauty.
By thy power and love it is so.

ENERGY BALANCING

In crystal healing the pattern of health is seen as intrinsically linked with energy balancing, acknowledging that in a sense we are all made of nothing but patterns of resonant energy formed by thought and interacting with the energies of the world about us and with the universe itself. Here are some simple but effective methods of energy balancing that you might like to try.

It is helpful at the outset to discover how you, and/or the person you are working with, are polarised. We all have a receiving side and a giving side, a minus or plus if you think in terms of electrical circuitry, with which we take in energy and send it out. While most often applied to the hands, this concept actually applies to the body as a whole.

You will find that your giving hand (or + charge) is very often the same as the hand you write with, your other hand (or — charge) being the more receptive and sensitive one. Both sending and receiving energy are essential to life and by balancing these two impulses a healthy life flow can be restored. It is possible that your polarity can switch at times of life changes, extreme stress or trauma, and so it is not always safe to assume your dominant hand is the same side as your giving hand (outgoing energy). A good way to check which way you are polarised is to use a natural quartz point.

DISCOVERING YOUR POLARITY
Rub your hands together briskly, take a (cleansed) natural quartz crystal in your left hand, point outwards, and gently comb your right palm from your wrist to the finger tips, keeping the point about 5 mm away from the surface of your skin. Allow yourself to be relaxed and quietly receptive and you will start to experience some small physical sensation, a breeze perhaps, heat or cold, maybe even a slight prickling, as the crystal passes over the surface of your palm. This is a subtle but distinct effect. When you get a reaction, switch your crystal into your right hand and repeat the process, this time over your left palm. The hand which senses the crystal most strongly will be your receiving hand (or — charge), also

indicating your receiving side. The other less sensitive hand is your giving (or + charge) hand and side. Once you have established your polarity you can easily re-balance your energy with a single natural quartz point as described below.

YOUR AURA

Your aura (from the Greek, meaning 'breeze' or 'breath') is the name often given to your personal energy field — all living things have one — and it can be easily detected at a simple level as the heat that radiates from your body. Apart from heat generated by the body, the aura contains or reflects increasingly subtle permeable layers (or fields) of energy within your sphere of influence, from the purely physical such as heat and cold, through various positive and negative emotional and mental states, to the most subtle, spiritual condition of being pure essence. It is the emotional forces, due to our experience and our response to life, carried within the energy field that influence the physical tissues of the body. In a very real sense, to borrow Dr Caroline Myss's helpful description: 'Your biography becomes your biology.'

There are some safe and simple methods for using crystals to help correct imbalance or damage in the aura which will affect the clarity of your emotional response to life experiences — although the effects of trauma, beliefs, social and family attitudes and behaviours etc. will have already shaped (mostly unconsciously) patterns of thinking and behaviour. Ideally, crystal work of this sort would go hand in hand with seeking a greater understanding and consciousness of yourself, so that destructive patterns can be released.

When using crystals to balance the aura, always apply the basic principles of first clearing and/or cleansing followed by boosting or re-energising. Working within a sacred space in the form of one of the crystal grids outlined in Chapter 6 will give you the benefit of a good, clear environment in which to clear, re-balance and energise your aura. Be sure to only use cleansed and charged crystals.

Quartz points used with the point directed away from the body will 'clear' and draw off excess or imbalanced eneregy. Quartz points directed towards the body will tend to introduce energy into the aura or (in a geometric grid) create a contained energy field.

AURA CLEARING

Using one natural quartz point, hold your crystal in the palm of your *giving* hand (+) with the point directed away from the body, towards your middle finger-tip. You can assist the work of the crystal by focusing on your breathing. Breathe in, allowing your body to relax, while visualising pure clean air/light/life force filling you. Concentrating on your out-breath, imagine as you exhale that you are letting go of all the disharmony, fear, pain and tiredness that you might be holding. Repeat this gentle breathing until you feel free and clear. This is only the first stage of your energy balancing and you will know when you are clear, as it will leave you feeling rather empty and drained.

ENERGY BOOSTING

Once clear, you need to boost your energy with clarity and vitality. Simply move the crystal across into your *receiving* hand, the point now directed towards your wrist, into your body. Use your breathing again, this time imagining that you are breathing in pure sparkling white light and, on your out-breath, that you are sending this pure air/light/life force to every cell and atom of your body to boost and protect your whole energy field. Repeat this light breathing for a few minutes until you feel calm and energised.

TWO CRYSTALS

You can combine clearing and boosting in one exercise by using two quartz points at the same time, one in each hand — one quartz point in your giving hand, point away from the body, and the other crystal in your receiving hand, point towards your body. By releasing tiredness, pain and fear etc. on the out-breath and filling yourself with pure light on the in-breath, you will quickly create a balanced energy circuit. You could also place another two crystals at the feet, or just work via the feet if preferred. Balancing your aura in this way will leave you feeling refreshed and energised and is a great pick-me-up at the end of a busy day.

MAPPING YOUR ENERGY

In Eastern traditions the flow and interaction of universal energy or life force has been charted, showing its interplay with body, mind and spirit. The most famous of these maps shows the Chinese acupuncture meridians, which details the flow of *ch'i* energy through the body via channels and points (rather like an alternative circulatory system), and the Hindu *chakra* system, which describes a series of wheels or vortexes located within the aura. These *chakras* each act as a multilevelled interface that enables and regulates the flow of energy, incoming and outgoing, between the individual and the universe, via different subtle energetic influences and emanations, from pure energy into dense matter. These invisible centres of spinning energy receive, transmit and transform energy (functions that are reflected in the energetic properties of crystals) at social/physical, sexual, emotional, mental and spiritual levels.

The *chakra* map that I use describes a basic pattern of seven major energy centres which are found within the aura. I find it especially useful as it can be associated with the seven colours of the light spectrum. It provides a symbolic balance that is helpful in meditation and self-healing and is a good basis for crystal work. These centres are listed with their approximate physical locations and some of their common associations, influences and colours:

1. Base or root chakra (red and black) — located at base of the spine/pubic bone (or, according to some systems, at the perineum between genitals and anus). Associated with earth, your foundation, the instinctual nature, the material world, material concerns and welfare etc. In correspondence with the adrenals, spinal column and the kidneys.

2. Sacral chakra (orange) — located on the body's midline, four finger widths below the navel. Associated with sexuality, nourishment and emotion. This centre is divided in some systems, sex and emotion. In correspondence with the gonads and the reproductive system.

3. Solar plexus chakra (golden yellow) — located at the solar plexus. Associated with personal power, will, self-confidence, action. In correspondence with the pancreas, stomach, liver, gall bladder and nervous system.

4. Heart chakra (green) — located on the midline, level with the heart. Associated with unconditional love, self-acceptance, the movement from the purely personal to wider care and concern for others, free from attachments or expectations. In correspondence with the thymus, heart, blood, circulation.

5. *Throat chakra (sky blue)* — located on the throat. Associated with self-expression, communication of all kinds, creativity. In correspondence with the thyroid, bronchials, lungs, alimentary canal.

6. *Brow or third eye chakra (indigo)* — located between the eyebrows. Associated with mental thought, intuition and psychic development. In correspondence with the pituitary, lower brain, left eye, ears, nose, nervous system.

7. *Crown chakra (violet > white)* — located at the crown of the head. Associated with spirituality, connection with the godhead, the life force, the universal and cosmic energies. In correspondence with the pineal, upper brain, right eye.

It's important to remember that this is only a map, a representation of the territory, not the territory itself. In order to explore your own energetic territory, you might like to read Dr Caroline Myss's book *Anatomy of the Spirit* for its penetrating and useful insights or use the *chakra* balance exercise on page 121 and give thought to where you sense disturbance or pain within yourself — a crystal well placed can help you to become sensitive and aware and also help to ease and unblock emotional pain. This will bring greater harmony to the energetic flow to your whole being.

CHAKRA STONES

You might like to make up your own *chakra* set of crystals from among the following (check the Directory for more information on each stone):

Base: red and black stones — obsidian (Apache tears), hematite, smoky quartz, garnet, ruby, jasper

Sacrum: carnelian, rhodochrosite or orange calcite
Solar plexus: citrine, topaz, gold tiger eye, sunstone or
yellow calcite
Heart: green jade, emerald, malachite, aventurine,
watermelon tourmaline, rose quartz or amazonite
Throat: blue lace agate, blue chalcedony, turquoise or
fluorite
Brow: azurite, lapis lazuli, dumortiorite, celestite, sodalite
or hawk's eye
Crown: clear quartz, sugilite, selenite, white calcite or
amethyst

PAIN RELIEF

Another invaluable use for crystals in healing is their
remarkable ability to relieve pain, gently and completely non-
invasively. This does not necessarily mean that the physical
condition — arthritis is a good example — is cured by the
crystal, but that pain is definitely eased by placing crystals on
the affected area. Refer to the *Colour Crystal Directory* at
the end of the book for details of specific healing properties,
but I would say that one of the crystals from the quartz group
should give you the help you need. Place the crystal on the
painful area, directly on the skin or on top of a natural
material such as cotton, and leave it there until relief is felt. If
it is comfortable to do so, you could hold a small crystal in
place with a strip of micropore surgical tape. My father gets
great relief in his arthritic knees by using two small crystal
points, one on each knee, directed away from the body.

GEM WATERS AND GEM ELIXIRS

The subtlest — but very powerful — way of using crystals for healing is the use of gem elixirs. These are remedies made from spring or distilled water that has been charged with specific crystals and gemstones. They are particularly good for treating negative mental and emotional states and for shifting long-term, ingrained attitudes and conditioning that are hindering your growth. With practice you can learn to feel the presence of the elixir and differentiate between different gems and their effects.

N.B. Gem elixirs are outside the Medicines Act in the UK, which states that it is illegal to claim a product is beneficial in treating a physical ailment without its having undergone successful clinical trials and the subsequent granting of a licence.

WHAT YOU NEED
Crystals and gemstones, preferably in their natural state, although tumbled stones will do[1]

spring or distilled water
glass jars or glasses
brandy[2]
glass dropper bottles sterilised in boiling water
labels

After you have cleaned and charged your gemstones, you can make *gem water* (also called structured water) or *gem elixir* (also called tinctures, remedies and essences). This is an excellent way to learn about the gemstones and to discover how the stones work with your own energies. The properties of the individual stones will give you some idea as to how the essences might work for you. You should always keep a record of how you are feeling when you are taking a gem essence and any changes that occur. I would strongly recommend that you learn about the effects of the gem elixirs on yourself before giving them to anyone else. If you are serious about studying this aspect of crystal healing, I strongly recommend *Gem Elixirs and Vibrational Healing* (2 volumes) by Gurudas for a most comprehensive guide.

GEM WATER

1. Sterilise a glass jar by pouring boiling water into it, then place the cleansed stone inside. If you are making gem water, use a large jar such as a pickling jar. You can use something much smaller for essences.
2. Add spring or distilled water.
3. Cover the container (with plain glass ideally) and place it on a natural surface (grass, earth, wood) outside in the sun for several hours or, even better, for twenty-four hours at full moon to get the benefit of sun and moon. Moon energies are good for emotions.
4. Bless the water. For example, you could say a favourite prayer of thanksgiving or you could tune in to the nature spirits (devas) with love and gratitude and ask their help in charging the water for healing.
5. Store in stoppered bottles in a cool place, ideally in the fridge.

Gem water lasts for two or three days at most. Gem waters are especially suitable for treating animals and plants.[3]

GEM ELIXIR STOCK

If you wish to use the remedy on an ongoing basis, you must preserve it as an elixir in the following way:

1. Sterilise a brown dropper bottle (with glass dropper), usually available from your local pharmacy.
2. Fill the bottle halfway with the gem water.
3. Fill the rest of the bottle with brandy. Now you have an essence which is 50 per cent water and 50 per cent alcohol.
4. Label the bottle as 'stock' e.g. 'ruby stock' and store on a cool shelf out of the sunlight. If you have made several, store them separately making sure that the bottles are not touching.

DOSING BOTTLE

You can take the elixir either by putting five drops from the stock into a glass of spring water and sipping at intervals through the day or by making up another dropper bottle of the diluted elixir to carry with you:

1. Sterilise another dropper bottle and fill one-third full of brandy.
2. Top up with spring water and add 2–5 drops of your stock and shake.
3. Label it e.g. 'ruby elixir' to differentiate it from your stock bottle.
4. Take drops under your tongue or in water at intervals.

If you re-use bottles, be sure to sterilise them well, especially the droppers. Boiling for 20 minutes is good practice. Little and often is a better way of dosing than lots all at once. *You can become overcharged with gem essences* and obvious signs of spaciness or dizziness will let you know this is the case and you should stop. Use common sense and do not drive or operate machinery until the symptoms have disappeared.

CRYSTALS FOR PETS

Crystal waters, made as described above, are not only excellent for treating humans but also very effective for treating
animals and plants. If you have a sick animal it is, of course,
most important that you seek the immediate advice of your
vet, but crystals can bring about an energy balance that will
speed recovery. You can do this in several ways — by making
the appropriate crystal water (see the *Colour Crystal
Directory* at the end of this book for the properties of
individual crystals) and adding a few drops to the drinking
bowl, or you could place a small piece of rose quartz or other
crystal in, under or near the animal's bed. Or, if the animal
will stay still for you, you might create a crystal grid, such as
the Star of David (see Chapter 6) around your pet. Yet
another way would be to make a little healing grid around a
photograph of the animal, so that he or she is receiving a
form of absent healing.

For ways of using crystals to encourage healthy plants
and to give a boost to ailing ones, (see Chapter 15). For
further information about crystal healing and information
about using crystals with the *chakra* system, see my book,
Healing with Crystals.

CHAPTER 7

Crystals and Communal Living

*If we live in peace with ourselves, we in turn may bring
peace to others.
A peaceable man does more good than a learned one.*

Thomas à Kempis

If you have the luxury of a little preparation time ahead of
your move, it's a really good idea to draw a good ground
plan of your new home, indicating the site in relation to the
compass directions and major environmental influences (is it
next door to a power station or a pub perhaps?) and the
position of its doors, windows, fireplaces, electrical power
points and other fixtures. This will give you a skeleton on which
you can build and should indicate any potential problems.

Even if you are not about to move, this is a useful exercise
to apply to your home as it helps you to consider elements
you may have overlooked or areas that have evolved out of
habitual patterns which you might like to change. Don't
despair — some degree of muddle or conflict is almost
inevitable in spaces regularly shared by two or more people.

You'll need to take into account the personalities
involved — if you are an eager collector of ephemera, you
will not be comfortable in an environment of pared-back
minimalism. Indeed, what is restful for some can cause acute
stress in others. Plenty of discussion at the outset, with a
view to seeking common goals and fulfilling mutual needs, is
vital along with willingness, humour and compromise,
compromise, compromise.

ASPECT AND ENVIRONMENT

Is there a view to enjoy, a wonderful world outside that you want to link with your home, or is your home a secret oasis behind firmly closed doors? Consider the environment and whether or not it is a benefit or a problem for you. Not every country setting is idyllic, nor every urban one a jungle. Beautiful countryside can be scarred by electrical pylons, landfill and motorways. Cities can feel threatening, or vibrant with their own special energy and charm. If you are lucky you will have an environment you enjoy which can offer some extra dimension to your home. Make a note of what you consider to be the pluses and minuses of your site.

Even if you have decided to do some work on your existing home, think about the approach to your house. Do you have control of the immediate surroundings by owning the space around the house or do you share a communal space with neighbours — maybe a path, hallway or stairs? What aspects do you like and what would you like to change?

You may be aware of possible geopathic stress affecting areas of your home — common signs are cold patches within a room or rooms that always feel cold despite heating, disturbed sleep and rapid deterioration of health and vitality, especially obvious in small children and the elderly. This can be easily checked with a hand-held compass and any problems successfully tackled with the careful placing of crystals (see Chapter 6 for details).

THE EIGHT DIRECTIONS

It is helpful to work with the compass directions in relation to your home. Each direction has different elemental associations and these can be used to encourage positive influences to work within your home. You will notice that the five elements in *feng shui* differ somewhat from the traditional Western elemental attributions.

Great importance is given to the positive and negative effects of one element on another — *water* is seen as the element of biological origin, it nourishes *wood*, symbolising growth, which becomes more active close to *fire*, which it feeds. Pulsing and active, fire turns into ash which nourishes the *earth* and the gathering quality of the soil. Eventually earth hardens into *metal* and the force is solidification. As well as the transformation and creativity expressed in this picture, there are also built-in checks and balances, bringing control — thus, water controls fire, wood controls earth, fire controls metals, earth controls water and metal controls wood.

I have given both Western and *feng shui* elemental attributions and you will need to decide what feels most comfortable to you. If you wish to go into *feng shui* properly, I recommend you read one of the many excellent books on the market. There are some recommendations at the back of this book.

East is the direction of the rising sun, the element of air, of awakening, springtime, children, new ideas, adventures and fresh starts.
In *feng shui* this is the direction for family and health matters. The *feng shui* symbol for this direction is the tree/wood, therefore woody greens and browns are believed to bring special blessings.
Stones — fluorite, calcite, apophyllite, aventurine, amazonite, amethyst, rose quartz, celestite and copper.

South-east — In *feng shui* this is the direction that benefits wealth and prosperity and this is enhanced by green. Also attributed to the tree/wood element, a money tree in this corner will double fortunate influences.

South is the direction of the noonday sun, the element of fire, summer, inspiration, creativity, enterprises, passion, youth and vigour.
In *feng shui* south is the direction of the element of fire, recognition and fame, all energised and activated by the colour red.
Stones — citrine, clear and rutilated quartz, Herkimer diamond, fire agate, ruby, garnet, carnelian, sunstone, gold.

South-west — In *feng shui* this is the direction associated with marriage and romantic relationships, the earth/soil elements, and the most auspicious colour is yellow. A piece of rose quartz will bring special blessings when placed in this area of your home.

West is the direction of the setting sun, the element of water, the emotions, autumn, meditation, maturity, mourning, release, change and transformation.
In *feng shui* this is the direction of children and the element is metal. Best colours for this direction are metallic, white and gold.
Stones — aquamarine, blue chalcedony, blue lace agate, labradorite, opal, moonstone, jade, silver.

North-west — In *feng shui* this is also the direction of metal. This direction benefits mentors, helpful friends and networking, and the colours that will enhance this influence are metallic, white and gold.
Stones — white quartz, rutilated quartz, gold.

North is the direction of darkness, night, the element of earth, withdrawal, winter, sleep and death.

In *feng shui* this is the direction of water and it benefits your career prospects, and the colours black and blue will emphasise this.

Stones — azurite, sodalite, smoky quartz, clear quartz, obsidian, snowflake obsidian, black tourmaline, jet, hematite, iron.

North-east — In *feng shui* this is the direction for soil/ earth and for education and knowledge. The colours are cream and beige.

THE CENTRE

The centre is the heart, the still point on which the world turns, the place of soul, essence, the cauldron of regeneration, spiritual nourishment, encounter and presence. Find the heart in your home and make it a place of beauty and honour.

In *feng shui* the centre is called the *Tai Ch'i*, and is seen as the pivotal source of radiance and energy for the home.

A really beautiful clear quartz cluster or a luminous crystal sphere would be a good choice for this location. A rainbow quartz sphere, for example, will send its light and joy in all directions influencing the whole house or apartment. A large piece of rose quartz is another possibility. Keep it simple. One fine crystal is infinitely better that lots of different crystals which can set up a confusing energy 'chatter'.

THE FOUNDATIONS

If you are planning to build a new house you might like to use crystals when laying the foundations as Melody, one of my neighbours, did recently. She chose four equal-sized clear quartz points for the four corners beneath the house, points directed inwards towards the centre (for details of the Cross-quarter and other grids, see Chapter 5), and she chose a piece of rough rose quartz for the centre — this grid will create a beautifully warm and balanced energy — the laser strength of the clear quartz softened by the radiance of the rose which it amplifies at the centre. Remember to cleanse, bless and dedicate these special stones so that they carry this blessing through into the very fabric of the new home.

RITUAL TO ESTABLISH THE HEART OF THE HOME
When you make a ritual it is a good idea to choose a day and time of special significance to you, or when there is a power-ful moon (waxing), a solstice or other festival to lend its energy to your intention.

You will need:

- Plant mister
- Clear quartz gem water
- A crystal (to remain as the focus and transmitter of energy at the centre of the space)
- Incense or smudge with small heat-proof container
- Matches
- A white candle
- A cup or chalice of water
- Flowers or small plant
- A small table or cloth

Thoroughly clean the whole area in the usual ways. Take a shower or bath yourself and change into freshly laundered clothes. Using a plant mister, spray the whole area lightly with clear quartz gem water, especially in corners and around doorways. Place the table or cloth over the place you have decided is the heart of your home. Place the incense to the east, the candle to the south, the water to the west and the flowers in the north. Light the incense and the candle.

Next, as you place the crystal at the centre, recite one of these dedication blessings or a blessing of your own. Visualise the energies of love, light and peace radiating to the furthest corners and extent of your home as you speak the words of dedication:

> *Love be in my heart and in my home.*
> *Light be in my heart and in my home.*
> *Peace be in my heart and in my home.*

or

> *May the heart of my home be a centre of love,*
> *Love that engenders warmth and sympathy.*
> *May the heart of my home be a centre of light,*
> *Light that shines with power and energy.*
> *May the heart of my home be a centre of peace,*
> *Peace that nurtures understanding and wisdom.*

> *May the love, light and peace in my home touch the*
> *hearts of all who enter here.*

You may like to sit in quiet attunement for a few minutes, letting the meaning of your words take root. Sense the radiance that has been established and how it reaches out to embrace your whole home. If it is safe to do so, you might leave the incense and candle alight for the rest of the day or evening. When you are ready to close, remove everything but the crystal and give thanks.

THRESHOLDS

Who comes to me, I keep
Who goes from me, I free
Yet against all I stand
Who do not carry my key
Threshold Blessing

Thresholds have always carried a deep significance and the threshold of your home is no different. It is the place of moving from the inner, private world to the outer, public arena, and it is across this threshold that guests are invited. Inevitably, significant changes of energy are involved in this movement, and while the door (and its lock) represents the physical barrier that must be negotiated, there are things we can do to ease the transition.

When we go out we usually *put on* outdoor clothes — suitable footwear for the weather and temperature, an overcoat against the cold, a mac if it is raining, a straw hat against a burning sun. When we come home we *take off* this outer wear. In many cultures, shoes are left at the door and house slippers are worn. This serves the practical function of not walking dirt into the house as well as the subtler value of not transferring the chaotic energies of the outer world to the sanctuary of the home. The holy water font beside the front door of Catholic homes is a beautiful tradition which acknowledges the need of sacred protection at the threshold.

The use of an amethyst cluster, with its powerful clearing and protective properties, as an energy cleaner just inside the front door will have the double benefit of clearing the incoming energy (imagine being washed by a shower of violet light) while enveloping those who leave in a clean bubble of protective crystal energy. Inside our front door we have a little fountain in which a large amethyst cluster is constantly washed by the streaming water — the positive energy it broadcasts is palpable.

HALLWAYS, STAIRS AND LANDINGS

Transitional spaces such as hallways, stairs and landings should be kept as clear of clutter as possible with the careful placing of certain helpful elements to slow down very fast-moving energy or *ch'i*, especially where a front and back door face each other at each end of the hall or corridor. A typical *feng shui* cure might be to place wind chimes in the hallway or on the stairwell as they moderate the *ch'i* where different energies converge or change — outdoors to indoors, a space with lots of doorways, or downstairs to upstairs. The use of a large plant as a partial screen to break up a long straight passageway will slow down the flow of *ch'i* especially where there are facing doors — the idea is for energy to flow harmoniously through the home, not for it to race in and straight out again like a dart.

A labradorite (merlin stone) sphere would be a good choice for assistance in easing transitions, changing levels and bringing clear-sightedness to your chosen path or direction as symbolised by the transitional spaces in your home.

KITCHENS

Celtic Prayer
Be gentle when you touch bread
Let it not lie, uncared for, unwanted.
So often bread is taken for granted.
There is such beauty in bread —

Beauty of surf and soil,
Beauty of patient toil.
Wind and rain have caressed it,
Christ often blessed it.
Be gentle when you touch bread.

Kitchens, like bathrooms, are functional, working spaces and while hygiene, practicality and safety are priorities, this should in no way prevent there being a strong sense of enjoyment and nurture as well.

Cooks Blessing
With a grateful and loving heart I prepare this food

Crystals are most useful in the kitchen for clearing imbalanced energy fields, such as background radiation from electrical appliances, and for creating the right ambience for preparing food. Clear or smoky quartz clusters and points are the best choices for clearing background radiation around electrical appliances. Check your appliances with a hand-held compass to see if any electrical field disturbance is present (for details of this technique, see Chapter 5, page 37). Be sure there's a need before adding these crystals — remember, if it ain't broke, don't fix it! Rose quartz will bring its special blessing to the preparation of food as well as inspiring extra creativity.

There are some *feng shui* principles which you could find helpful when applied to your own kitchen layout. In *feng shui* terms the kitchen, where food is prepared and life sustained, is seen as the source of wealth and well-being in the home and as such is the most important room in the house. The stove should not be either next to or directly opposite the sink, as fire and water need to be balanced and apart, but not in opposition. Ideally the stove should be in a corner or supported by two walls, allowing at least a partial view of the door — which gives the cook a greater sense of security and control over the space. Neither should the stove be under a window or skylight, as in this position the energy of the food will be lost rather than benefiting the inhabitants.

As well as avoiding having the stove beside the sink, you should also keep it a distance from the refrigerator, for the same reason. A popular way to ease the energy between hot/cold, fire/water is to hang a small plant in the space between, so that the energy then flows from water to wood to fire. Even a painting of plants or woods in this position would bring greater harmony. The ideal placement for the stove is facing east or south in the northern hemisphere (north in the southern hemisphere), towards the light.

EATING AREAS

A Food Blessing
We give heartfelt thanks
For the gift of life
And the blessings we receive
From the life of the earth

Whether your eating area is part of the kitchen or a separate room, it should be as peaceful and calm as possible, clear and harmonious, for the really good assimilation of the food. A large mirror placed in such a way that the table is reflected will double the abundance and benefits of the food placed on it. Citrine placed in the eating area will promote good digestion and, through its influence on the root *chakra*, radiate feelings of comfort, confidence and optimism. Rose quartz and amethyst would also be good choices for harmony in the eating area.

BATHROOMS

Bathrooms can be beautiful as well as functional spaces, making a benefit of the requirements for hygiene and practicality. Consider the space available to you and the needs it must fulfil. Young families will certainly have specific needs and where there are small children, safety must be a special consideration. Because the bathroom is a place for clearing and cleansing, it is a really good idea to get rid of any clutter and tidy away bottles, medicines and jars into a cupboard.

The lines of your bathroom should be clean and simple so that the overall effect is airy and avoids stagnation. For the same reason good ventilation will reduce heaviness and humidity. Plenty of light is essential as light is energy and this will stimulate *ch'i* in the room — if you don't have a strong natural light source, then recessed halogen down lights are very effective. Mirrors are especially helpful where you have no window, as they will add a sense of space, reflect light and speed up the *ch'i*, once again preventing stagnation. Soft blinds or curtains will soften the hard effect of stone or tiled flooring.

Ideally the lavatory should be hidden from view or as far away from the door as possible, and as an extra precaution the bathroom door should be kept closed to shield the rest of the house. *Feng shui* practitioners recommend keeping the lavatory seat down and the bath plug in to prevent energy being drained away. There is a tendency for 'water rooms' to wash away beneficial energy from the home (a bathroom in the south-eastern section of the house, for example, might be draining wealth from the home), so green plants in the bathroom are especially helpful. This is because, in Eastern elemental terms, the plant (wood) feeds on water, thereby reducing the draining effect. Plants will also absorb the humidity of a steamy bathroom and thrive in the process.

A bright, light-reflecting crystal such as a good clear quartz cluster is ideal for bathrooms.

LIVING-ROOMS

The living-room should be comfortable, welcoming, warm and well lit. This room usually gets plenty of use and often has to cope with a variety of needs, some possibly conflicting. In this case you might consider a cross-quarter grid (see page 39) of clear quartz points to bring harmony and balance to the overall space. Another possibility, especially if you want to instil tranquillity, would be a large, display-quality amethyst cluster which not only looks wonderful but radiates its calm and protective energy through the room, influencing all those using it. If you have a television in this room, it's a good idea to check for electrical radiation (see page 37) and static — if so, a clear quartz point or cluster on top of the set will ease the problem.

In *feng shui* the living-room represents family life, your personal history and culture, so it is the ideal place for displaying your special treasures — art and mementoes of personal significance and self-expression. Special attention should be paid to comfortable seating where your family and guests will feel safe and secure. This means that where you sit needs to be protected from behind, either by a wall or by using a display of plants on a small table or bookcase, to prevent a sense of floating alone in the middle of the room. Seats are better in groupings along with other furniture — small side and end tables can lend extra stability by anchoring the seating. As a general rule in *feng shui* it is best not to sit with your back to the main door.

If you have the space, you can treat the living-room as a microcosm for your whole home, acknowledging the different influences of various sectors of the room — family, children, relationships etc., each honoured in their appropriate place with the choice of colours, plants and crystals, consciously benefiting and reflecting these aspects of your life (see the attributions for the eight directions at the beginning of this chapter). Rose quartz is a good general choice in the living-room, bringing a sense of love, warmth, friendliness and well-being.

MIRRORS: A REFLECTION OF OURSELVES

Mirrors serve many functions in the creation of a healthy home. Practical mirrors for checking the appearance, doing make-up, shaving or brushing hair are very frequently too small, reflecting small bits of the whole. It is good to remember that you are larger, much more extensive than your physical self, and any mirror that does not also reflect at least six inches of the aura as well as your face is not a true reflection of what you are. A dressing mirror should equally reflect back to you more than your physical body. Remember also that guests may be taller than you, so make sure your mirrors take this into account.

Mirrors should be clean, not cracked, untarnished and well framed with soft rather than hard edges (which can be unconsciously cutting) to increase the sense of expansion and light. Mirrors that join in a corner produce a distorted reflection that can be countered by putting a large pot plant into the corner.

Mirrors enable energy to flow. Placed either side of an entrance, they can greatly increase the flow of new energy into your life. Equally, a well-placed mirror will expand and open up cramped and enclosed spaces, allowing energy blocks to be released and adding depth and light. This is useful in L-shaped rooms — place a large mirror on the two inner walls of the L to open up the 'missing' corner (see diagram below).

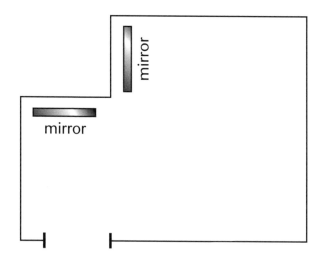

Mirrors used in L-shaped rooms (to open up 'missing' corner)

Round convex mirrors have traditionally been used in hallways for their light and energy-spreading effect. Always make sure mirrors are reflecting something pleasing or worthwhile because whatever is reflected is amplified.

Hanging a silvered glass ball (sometimes called a 'witch ball' — its ability to reflect the whole room was presumably useful for revealing any lurking witches!) is an alternative to using a mirror where cutting lines of energy, such as a long facing street, lamp-post or tall tree, are pointing directly at an entrance or window. An ideal place for this would be just inside the entrance, aligned with the door, or hanging in the window.

INDOOR WATER FEATURES

Indoor fountains and water features can be used to great effect wherever you want to bring more life and vitality. If you are following *feng shui* principles you would choose areas in the home that are compatible with, or stimulated by water. Crystals and water have a great affinity — flowing water energises crystals, ensuring the crystals do not become depleted. A fountain incorporating crystals in an entrance hall or stairwell brings a strong clean energy that sets the tone of the home.

There are lots of ready-made water features to choose from, but if you are feeling creative you can make something completely unique with a simple bowl, a small electrical water pump (follow instructions carefully and check the pressure in the sink before its final positioning) and the crystals of your choice. Some good combinations might include: a glass or perspex bowl with a clear or steel pipe or straw to carry the water up to fountain over an amethyst or clear quartz cluster; rough rose quartz in a slate, pewter or brushed steel basin; lined wood with water plants and moss agates; or a bubble fountain through a single colour or rainbow mix of tumblestones.

CHAPTER 8

Crystals and Personal Space

Life is not a problem to be solved, but a mystery to be lived
Thomas Merton

Everyone needs privacy, but sometimes it can be hard to achieve. Even if you are sharing a very small living space, crystals can help give you that much-needed sense of personal space and protection. Whether or not you have your own room, you can create what I call sacred space, that is, a clear energy field around you either by wearing the right crystal as a pendant or by setting up an appropriate crystal grid. In Chapter 5 several grids are described, each suited to a specific purpose, but in this chapter I will outline those most suited to giving you a sense of self-contained peace. In addition, this chapter will give you specific suggestions for treating a variety of personal spaces — from where you sleep to where you study. (Meditation and creating meditation spaces is treated in Chapter 17.

DEFINING PERSONAL SPACE: ENERGY FIELDS

Energy is what keeps us alive. It is a vital resource for all living functions, physical, emotional, mental and spiritual. Einstein said we are surrounded by a sea of energy, which he described as invisible, boundless and in perfect order. Physicists today define it as *zero point energy*, that is, the energy which exists prior to its materialisation in form. This energy was variously described by earlier scientists. The French doctor, Mesmer (from whom we get the expression 'mesmerism'), called it *animal magnetism*; Wilhelm Reich called it *orgone*; and in the nineteenth century Baron von Reichenbach called it *odic force*. And as well as this vast sea of energy, which I call 'life force', there is an individual energy field surrounding the human body — called the aura — in the shape of a gigantic egg.

The 'universal' or 'life force' energy seems identical to the *prana* of Hindu yoga or the *heavenly ch'i* of traditional acupuncture which the Chinese believe is manufactured in the sun. No modern scientist would argue against the proposition that our solar system, indeed the entire cosmos, is a sea of radiation. We know too that certain wavelengths — broadly those perceived as light and heat — are necessary for the continuation of life, and that specific aspects of the spectrum influence our well-being, such as when ultraviolet light reacts on the human skin to trigger the production of vitamin D.

During this century much work has been done to measure energy fields and it is increasingly clear that all life forms have personal energy fields or auras. Back in the 1930s a Yale professor, Dr Harold Saxton Burr, became interested in the electrical potential of living things and set up equipment which successfully detected electrical field phenomena associated with trees and other plants, many animals, including humans, and even slime moulds. He discovered that such fields are not static — a voltmeter attached to a tree will, for example, show fluctuations in response to light, moisture, storms, sunspots and phases of the moon.

Due to his research over the years, Burr came to believe in the existence of a *life field* which as Lyall Watson says, 'holds the shape of an organism just as a mould determines the shape of a pudding'. Even though they went a long way towards explaining one of the most persistent mysteries of cellular biology — how certain cells in your body 'know' how to grow into a kidney, while others grow into a brain — Dr Burr's theories were largely ignored by the scientific establishment throughout much of his working life.

It has long been evident that some sort of organising principle is involved in living matter and scientists have devoted much time and effort in a vain attempt to isolate chemical or other triggers of the process. Pancreatic tissue grafted on to your nose will never result in the growth of a new pancreas on your face. Sponges sieved through silk to separate their constituent cells will nevertheless re-form as they were before. More impressive still, the cells of *two different* sponges may be sieved and mixed together without disrupting the process — they will re-form as separate individuals. In the absence of anything better, Dr Burr's life field certainly seems to fit the bill.

KIRLIAN PHOTOGRAPHY

But the idea of an energy system associated with the human body goes a step further with the work of the Russian electrical engineer Semyon Kirlian and his wife Valentina. They actually photographed the energy field. They set up two metal plates to act as electrodes, with photographic film placed on one of them. When Kirlian put his hand between the plates and switched on a high frequency current, apart from receiving a severe burn, when the film was developed it showed an image of Kirlian's hand surrounded by a luminescent halo.

The Kirlians refined their techniques and eventually created the technology to develop a whole new branch of photography. They used the new technology to make a great many pictures. Those which involved living tissue — even plant tissue like a leaf — showed sparks and flares of energy in patterns as dramatic as they were beautiful. A dead leaf showed nothing of these patterns. When a portion of a leaf was torn or cut away, a ghostly image of the missing piece clearly showed.

Research projects using Kirlian photographs of human volunteers show that the aura effect varies in relation to a subject's mood and was also influenced by personality interactions: the Kirlian auras of young men brightened when a pretty woman entered the room.

In the Neuropsychiatric Institute at UCLA, California, the scientific team of Thelma Moss and Ken Johnson constructed Kirlian apparatus which showed energy flares emitted by the fingertips of faith healers as they exercised their art. There was also a discovered linkage with Chinese acupuncture in that many traditional acupuncture points show as small flares in a Kirlian photograph.

HARRY OLDFIELD

In Britain, Harry Oldfield has pioneered the use of Kirlian photography in the investigation of crystals. Among his many Kirlian experiments he showed the influence of quartz on living energy fields. Marked increases in the corona discharge of fingertips holding a crystal, and in the energy field of a leaf when placed beside a quartz point, were shown in repeated cases.

Oldfield has also broken new ground using Kirlian photography and electrographic techniques for diagnosing disease. His view is that magnetic fields can act therapeutically by enabling normal cells to influence positively the damaged cells next to them, returning them to their normal pattern. Certainly RNA and DNA are very sensitive to, and are modified by magnetic fields — radiation not only damages cells but can reverse abnormalities depending on the frequency of radiation applied.

Extensive investigation of Kirlian photography, electromagnetic fields, the idea of morphogenic fields (as developed by Rupert Sheldrake) and the concept that there is a pattern of wholeness in the living organism, even if part of the physical whole is removed (a holographic life pattern), has led Harry Oldfield to develop a whole system of electrocrystal therapy. The trained practitioner uses a device that utilises an applied electrical field, amplified by quartz crystals, to re-align imbalanced energy and promote healing. His results are as impressive as his ongoing research. He sees the pattern of health intrinsically linked with energy balancing and reiterates the view that we are made of nothing but patterns of resonant energy.

BALANCING YOUR ENERGY

If you accept that your energy field is affected by your health, your moods, the moods and energy of the people around you and by your environment, you will see that balancing all these elements is vital to well-being. Crystals, due to their ability to transform energy and their tendency always to return energy to balance, are invaluable in protecting your energy and your space.

You need to start by assessing your own energy, beginning with your most immediate personal space, your aura (for information about balancing the aura, see Chapter 6). Consider such things as your general health and energy levels, your moods, your sleep patterns and any obvious causes of stress, especially if it is ongoing. Dealing with specific health or emotional problems is beyond the scope of this book, but taking time to consider steps you might take to improve your overall energy is never wasted.

The Star of David is the very best grid for personal balancing. For a chair grid, take six cleansed single terminated quartz points. Place each one on the floor about 50 cm from the body, pointing inwards, one behind you at the centre, one in front between your feet, one aligned with each shoulder and one aligned with each knee. To extend the grid when you are lying down, you still place each quartz point about 50 cm from the body, pointing inwards, one above the head, one beneath the feet, one level with each shoulder and one level with each knee. This elongates the star but is equally effective.

WORDS OF POWER

Sometimes you may feel the need for special protection — when you are particularly vulnerable due to difficult conditions such as illness, loss or grief. The power of the spoken word is an age-old means of protection and our prayers carry our intent and empower our actions, as well as bearing the force of devout repetition through the ages by countless others. The Lord's Prayer remains one of the most effective forces for protection within a Christian framework. If this is your tradition, then you can do no better.

The following prayer was given by someone attending a crystal workshop in Dublin some years ago. It does the job beautifully.

A Cleansing Prayer
I bless you,
I heal you,
I release you,

I forgive you and set you free.
I call forth the channels of love,
of super-consciousness,
of the Christ light,
to envelope all energies which are in need
of being enlightened and freed.
Thank you God and so it is.

Other helpful words and prayers might include one of the following:

Imagine yourself bathed in light, as though standing under a bright shower, and that you breathe this light into you. As you do, say in your mind or out loud:

I am in the light
and the light is in me.
or
I am in God
and God is in me.
(these make perfect blessings to use before you go to sleep) or

I stand in circles of light
that nothing may cross.

(If you can visualise this as you say the words, so much the better.)

BEDROOMS
The bedroom should be a haven of beauty and relaxation. What you see around you just before you fall sleep will

influence your dream state and the quality of your sleep; therefore choose your colours, furnishings and pictures accordingly. Piles of clothes, dirty laundry and overflowing waste-paper will contribute to poor sleep patterns. The bedroom is for the recovery of energy and anything that might be considered draining should be well away from the bed. Ideally, desks, work-related items, televisions, computers and music systems should be out of the room altogether. The best situation for the bedroom is at the back of the house signifying retreat from the world and the stimulating energy that comes in at the front door.

The best location for the bed is opposite or diagonally opposite the door, so that you can see the whole room from the bed and all who enter. For the same reason the bed should not be behind the door. If there is a slanted ceiling or beam above the bed, it's a good idea to hang a light canopy of floaty material over the whole length and width of the bed to counteract 'cutting' or 'pressing' energy effects. Sharp 'cutting' edges should also be avoided on furniture around the bed and ideally the bed should not back against a window. If the bed stands away from the wall, any space at the head should not be used as a corridor as this will have a draining effect. Mirrors in the bedroom should be round or oval and should not be placed in a position where you can see your own reflection when lying in bed, as this can be disturbing to the sleeping spirit.

Rose quartz is a good gentle energy for the bedroom that will not interfere with sleep patterns. Make a four square grid with some medium-sized chunks to create an overall harmony and peace. If you are in a special relationship or wish to attract one, then according to *feng shui* you should place rose quartz in the relationships area of the room, in the south-west, along with a healthy round-leafed plant and perhaps a photograph of the beloved.

STUDIES AND QUIET ROOMS

If you have your own study I won't need to tell you how lucky you are! The study does not have to be a workspace but rather a haven of peace and calm where you can retreat and recharge your batteries. It is also possible to create this space as part of a larger room, perhaps with the help of some sort of divider or screen — even a large leafy plant will give you some privacy.

Protect this space with a four square grid of quartz crystals, one in each corner, points to the centre of the room (or study area). A round-leafed plant or a peace lily would also bring good energy to the space. Choose harmonious colours and keep the space as uncluttered as possible, bearing in mind that every item in the room carries its own energy and associations. Too many 'things' may prove distracting.

CHAPTER 9

Crystals for Children

Imagination is evidence of the divine
William Blake

hildren love crystals, not just because they are so beautiful,
but because they are more open and sensitive than most
adults to their effects. Indeed, many parents are first
introduced to crystals by children who have already started
their own collection of rainbow-coloured tumblestones.

INFANTS AND TODDLERS
Because babies are energetically very open and have a
developing (and sometimes very fragile) connection with the
physical plane of reality, it is important to be mindful of the
influences that are brought into their aura. Many crystals
have the effect of extending our awareness beyond ordinary
reality. For babies and young children their struggle is to
learn how to narrow and focus their awareness sufficiently to
become fully part of this world, losing their state of blissful
union with all life in the process (which we search to
rediscover ever after). So most crystals are not helpful in
assisting your baby's becoming fully adapted and grounded.

But there is one exception — rose quartz, the love stone.
It is the best crystal (and the only one I recommend) for
babies and very young children and it can be invaluable as a
bridge of love and comfort, easing the child into becoming
comfortably self-conscious. Gentle enough not to disturb the
child's own delicate energy balance, a little piece of rose

Polished radiance *(Chapter 3)* (from top left): *Rose quartz, amethyst and clear quartz pyramids, small rose quartz spheres, clear quartz sphere, smoky quartz pyramid, blue calcite sphere, clear and green quartz 'rainbow' sphere, snowy quartz and amethyst prisms, clear quartz and rose prisms, fluorite 'palm' stones, rose quartz sphere, labradorite sphere, clear prism and sphere, rose quartz and smoky quartz obelisks.*

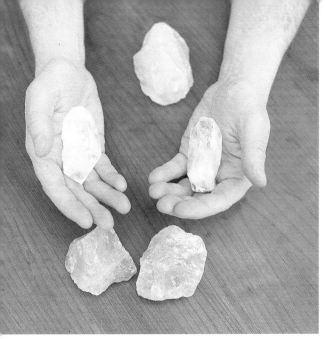

Energy balancing — circuit using two crystals (Chapter 6)

Healthy traveller's crystal kit (Chapter 10)

Heart of light *(Chapter 7): This large, clear quartz cluster with its fine, central, single point is ideal for generating energy at the heart of the home.*

Yellow, orange, red and black stones (from top left spiralling clockwise to centre): *Carnelian tumbles, tiger eye, black tourmaline 'schorl' and needles, rhodochrosite slice, tumbles and cabuchon, raw garnet and polished beads, citrine point and tumbles, obsidian egg and tumbles, ruby crystals, cut*

topaz and natural crystal, hematite tumbles, gold calcite 'stellar beam' crystal, orange calcite, 'snowflake' obsidian tumbles, smoky quartz tumbles, coral beads, smoky quartz polished 'prism', jasper tumbles, natural smoky quartz point.

Crystal protection — pendants and pendulums — on Winged Isis (from left): *Malachite, clear quartz, rose quartz, clear quartz with amethyst, rose quartz and jade beads, carved jade Kwan Yin with amethysts and moonstones, clear quartz sphere* (at knee), *blue lace agate, rainbow fluorite and opal, rose quartz, rainbow fluorite, clear quartz, clear quartz and lapis lazuli, amethyst, lapis lazuli.* 'Sunrays' (around agate slice) (from top left): *Clear quartz, citrine, purple fluorite, fluorite and opal, amethyst, clear quartz, fluorite, clear quartz (2), fluorite and clear quartz.*

Indigo and violet stones (from top left): *Purple fluorite octahedron and polished 'palm' stone, labradorite sphere and pebbles, amethyst tumbles, point, cluster and 'flower', azurite, amertrine sphere, lapis lazuli polished stones and egg, celestite natural clusters, three sugilite tumbles, quartz points of 'rose aura', 'acqua aura' and 'titania', sodalite* (centre).

A gentle way of clearing your crystals (Chapter 4)

Rose quartz plant reviver (Chapter 13): *Rose quartz in the pot of a plant that has suffered from a problem such as pest infestation or over- (or under-) watering will bring strength and a speedy recovery.*

quartz placed near or underneath the crib can soothe the trauma of a difficult birth. Rose quartz gem water (see Chapter 6 for details) rubbed gently on to the gums might be used to soothe the pain of teething.

Whenever there is the need for comfort, consolation, a lift of the spirits or the allaying of fear, rose quartz is invaluable. Harassed and sleep-deprived parents can also benefit from the influence of this beautiful stone for its calming and joyful influence, reconnecting you with the wonder and delight at the heart of parenting. Try a piece of rose quartz under the pillow for sweet dreams or in your pocket as you go about your day.

NIGHTMARES AND DISTURBED SLEEP

It is likely that your child will at some stage suffer from nightmares. While occasional bad dreams may be seen as a natural way of 'processing' challenging experiences and situations in waking life, frequent or recurring nightmares can leave the child afraid of going to sleep. One very effective way to help with this problem is to get into the habit of discussing the dreams of the family at breakfast each morning, especially encouraging the child or children to describe their own dreams, to see the power and the good in them (see details of the Senoi dream system in Chapter 16).

A small piece of rough rose quartz under the pillow is invaluable for bringing sweet dreams; amethyst (a small cluster beside or under the bed or a large tumblestone under the pillow) is particularly helpful as a protection from nightmares; and moonstone is recommended to prevent sleepwalking. The use of prayer before sleep is an age-old tradition which most children find comforting and protective. You do not have to use a specific religious framework in order to

create a blessing. Here are some examples of some
traditional, religious and non-religious blessings:

Bless me and keep me safe
All through the night
That I may wake in the morning
Happy to greet the new day.

May the moon and stars bless all my nights
And the sun bless all my days.

Traditional Christian Child's Prayer
Matthew, Mark, Luke and John
Bless the bed that I lie on
As I lay me down to sleep
I pray the Lord my soul to keep
And if I die before I wake
I pray the Lord my soul to take.

The Knight's Prayer
God be in my head, and in my understanding;
God be in my eyes, and in my looking;
God be in my mouth, and in my speaking;
God be in my heart, and in my thinking;
God be at my end, and at my departing.

Traditional Celtic Blessing
Deep Peace
Of the Running water
Deep Peace
Of the Flowing Air
Deep Peace

Of the Quiet Earth
Deep Peace
Of the Shining Stars
Deep Peace
Of the Son of Peace
To You

St Augustine's Prayer
Watch, O Lord, with those who wake, or watch, or weep
tonight,
And give your angels and saints charge over those who
sleep.
Tend our sick ones, O Lord Christ.
Rest your weary ones,
Bless your dying ones,
Sooth your suffering ones,
Pity your afflicted ones,
Shield your joyous ones,
And all for your love's sake.

Prayer of Yellow Lark, Chief of the Sioux Nation
O Great Spirit, whose voice I hear in the wind,
And whose breath gives life to all the world, hear me.
I come before you, one of your many children.
I am small and weak, I need your strength and wisdom.
Let me walk in beauty, and make my eyes behold the red
and purple sunset.
Make my hands respect the things you have made,
My ears sharp to hear your voice.
Make me wise, so that I may know the things you have
taught my people,
The lessons you have hidden under every leaf and rock.

I seek strength not to be superior to my sisters
and brothers,
But to be able to fight my greatest enemy — myself.
Make me ever ready to come to you with clean hands
and straight eyes,
So when life fades as a fading sunset,
My spirit may come to you without shame.

Project: Making a Dreamcatcher

Dreamcatchers have become very popular recently. They come from the native American tradition which believes that if you hang a dreamcatcher above your bed it will catch the bad dreams and only allow the good dreams to get through. You can buy a ready-made dreamcatcher quite easily, but it's really special to make your own.

You will need:

- a small wooden hoop (from a sewing or craft shop) or a very pliable stem (e.g. willow) that you can make into a hoop by binding the ends together with twine
- at least 2 metres of twine or thick fishing line
- some drilled crystal beads (available from a craft shop) e.g. clear quartz, rose quartz
- feathers or coloured ribbons

Begin by tying and knotting one end of your twine firmly to the hoop and then start your spider's web by making a further five or six equally spaced knots from the continuous thread right around the rim before working in towards the centre (see diagram). At intervals you can thread a little crystal bead on to your thread so that it is suspended in the net. When you get close to the centre, add another bead and tie off the thread. You can finish your dreamcatcher by binding the hoop with thongs or coloured ribbons and decorate it with feathers or by leaving some ribbon 'tails' hanging from what will be the bottom edge when it is hanging up.

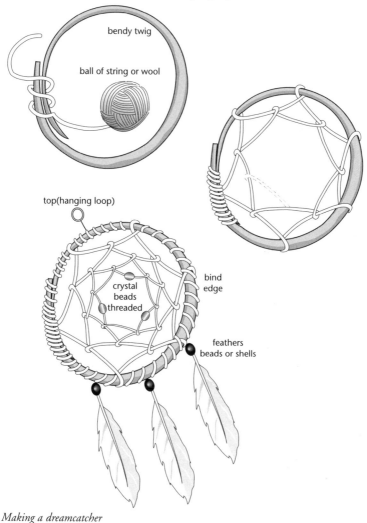

Making a dreamcatcher

CRYSTALS FOR CONFIDENCE

Imagination is one of our greatest gifts. Indeed, William Blake said that imagination is evidence of the divine. Yet, throughout our childhood, it is curbed and undermined as we are encouraged to narrow down our vision and awareness to a very limited and approved reality. Children are ridiculed for having invisible friends and many parents and teachers are ambivalent about how much they want children to believe in Santa Claus or the tooth fairy.

The loss of the magical in favour of being more 'grown up' before children are ready can lead to a profound disappointment and resignation because their sense of individual validity has been diminished — approval is so often reserved for compliance and uniformity, while imagination, the very source of creativity, is dismissed as fanciful, wool gathering or even untruthfulness.

Children have to deal with almost constant changes and transitions as they grow, all requiring adjustment. Some obvious examples include moving from a cot to a bed, coming out of nappies, the arrival of a new baby, going to school, making and losing friends, changing class (and teacher), learning to read/write/swim/ride a bike, increasing sexual awareness and the onset of puberty. At no other time in your life does so much happen and is so much expected of you. Increasingly complex emotional and social interactions are learned alongside creative play and schoolwork. And all the time the child is growing physically at a rate of several inches in a year. No wonder he or she is sometimes prey to fears and lack of confidence.

Troubled children sometimes wet their beds, which only adds to their distress, but the assistance of a rose quartz friend can give them invaluable support. The energy will bring a comforting protection and sense of security while helping them to find the confidence to express their needs and discuss their fears.

POCKET FRIENDS

Different crystal tumblestones can provide children with a range of helpers or 'pocket friends' that will support them through different stages of their lives. When carried in the pocket, these little crystals can become boon companions for the child, sharing fears and secrets and bringing their own special qualities of comfort and support.

A citrine or tiger's eye will connect with the child's own power and give extra confidence and courage, whether it be for a school test or for help in confronting some difficulty. Blue lace agate is de-stressing and calming. It will also help with communication and greater self-expression. Rose quartz will bring love, openness, empathy, comfort and happiness. Amethyst is very protective and will help with concentration and brings the child a strong spiritual connection. Moss agate will bring a close affinity with nature. Aventurine brings enthusiasm, light-heartedness, tolerance and a happy disposition. Aquamarine brings clarity and happiness. It can also help with travel sickness, allergies and nervous tummies. Carnelian is cheerful, warming and strengthening. Hematite brings strength and vitality and is protective and down to earth. Sodalite encourages individuality, freedom and self-expression. Clear quartz is very energising and protective.

Project: Making your Crystal a Talisman
A talisman is something made with the aim of assisting its owner in a specific way. You might like to help your child make a talisman for friendship, perhaps, or to provide

helpful psychological support when starting a new venture such as beginning or changing schools, classes or moving house. Be guided by your child for what he or she wants rather than what you think is needed and then make a little prayer or affirmation to say with your child and one of the above crystals. It is a good idea to keep it simply expressed and in the present tense.

Some examples might include:

- This crystal carries the blessing of friendship for _____ (*name of child*)
- This crystal carries the blessing of calm for _____ (*name of child*)
- This crystal carries the blessing of happiness for _____ (*name of child*)

RAINBOW COLLECTIONS

You might like to help your child make a rainbow collection of tumblestones. These are not only fun but can have a magical effect by balancing the *chakras* (for more information see Chapter 6). They can be pasted on to plain card or used to decorate pictures, boxes, shelves or furniture.

Project: Making a Healing Frame or Mirror

By arranging and gluing coloured tumblestones around a mirror or photo frame you will affect the energy of the person it reflects or whose photo it carries. This makes a lovely project which children can make themselves and a charming idea for Christmas or birthday presents. Use your imagination. Rose quartz, the love stone, would be lovely around a wedding portrait or photo of loved ones.

Tumblestones in rainbow colours could be arranged to bring the balance and healing of those colours, and a mirror surrounded by tumblestones would be very energising as well as being a cool addition to any room!

What you will need:

- A small plain mirror, picture or photo frame
- epoxy glue or similar, suitable for gluing stone and glass
- a selection of small tumblestones

Arrange the stones loosely on the frame to begin with, until you are happy with the way it looks, then glue the stones carefully following the instructions given with the glue. Leave the frame flat until the glue is completely set.

Crystals at Work

For most people about a third of their adult life is spent at work. We can be grateful for the current enthusiasm in *feng shui* practices for bringing awareness and some welcome changes to working environments and for the attention now drawn to Sick Building Syndrome as a fundamental cause of ill health. But this is still very new and by no means universal. For many the working environment as a source of disease and stress is barely acknowledged. There are also specific ways that crystals can help you deal with the negative elements of travelling which are outlined in this section.

CHAPTER 10

Travelling

Here be dragons
(an allusion to unexplored areas on some early maps)

Increasingly travel has become a part of daily life and effects on our health and energy levels reflect the stress involved. High volumes of traffic, be it on the ground or in the air, mean that pollution, anxiety and stress are for many a fact of everyday life. The world literally rushes past us, often leaving us dissociated and out of touch with the ground beneath our feet. We are told that 'God is in the details', yet long gone are the days when the infinite variety of life could be enjoyed at a walking pace, when the seasons determined our sleep patterns or climates and time zones changed only at the gentle pace of the 'Slow boat to China'. Many of our grandparents or great grandparents didn't travel beyond their own district from one year to the next.

While most of us cherish the expansion and freedom that modern transport gives us — and have lives and work geared to it — it is also vital for a healthy mind, body and spirit that we reconnect with nature's rhythms and sense our rootedness to the earth. One of the wonderful things about using crystals is that, while they link us with the energy of the earth, they are easily carried around. In this way you can support your own health and vitality and when you reach your destination — a strange hotel room, perhaps — you have the means of bringing your sacred space (a clean energy field) with you. You can set up a grid for the

room or the bed and be sure of healthy sleep and plenty of
energy.

COPING WITH FRUSTRATION

Ironically, ever increasing haste has meant we were never in
more need of developing patience. Anyone who has rushed
to catch a train only to hear an announcement of delays (or
worse) will know how difficult it is to remain calm in the
face of frustration. Although frustration is the common
symptom of life in the fast lane, appointments and plans
continue to be made according to a belief in the efficiency of
speed, usually the triumph of hope over experience. And, of
course, it's not just public transport that causes upset and
delay: your car can break down and even your bike can get a
puncture. But while you cannot improve the efficiency of the
trains, you can take steps to change your own relationship
with them and the world around you:

- Evaluate your life on a regular basis
- Give more time to what is really important to you
- Make contingency plans
- Learn some breathing and relaxation techniques
  and use them (see Chapter 17)
- Carry or wear some rose quartz
- Accept what you can't change
- If you are delayed, make new friends
- Pay attention to your surroundings
- Discover the meaning in your delay

CRYSTALS IN YOUR CAR

Road rage is a horrifying expression of uncontrolled frustration at the wheel — sometimes with fatal consequences.

It can happen to anyone. An aptly named snarl-up can turn a sweet old lady into an abusive monster. Help to avoid becoming a highway Mr or Ms Hyde with a piece of rose quartz in your car. It will ease tension and dissipate aggression, bringing much needed perspective, soothing and calm, but remember to cleanse your crystal at the end of the day. An air-ioniser is also a good addition to the car, helping to keep you fresh and alert and cutting down pollution.

CRYSTAL TRAVEL KIT
Crystals are blessedly portable and every traveller should consider the benefit of a basic kit containing four small travelling crystals — single quartz points. They will provide you with the wherewithal of creating a pristine clear space wherever you find yourself — hotel room, temporary office, tent or holiday home. By setting up a four square grid (see page 39) you can combat everything from power socket radiation and geopathic stress to uncomfortable emotional atmospheres that might be present in hotel rooms and strange environments. When you consider the turnover of guests passing through most hotels, it is not surprising that you might have some difficulty settling in this busy energy field and getting a good night's sleep, no matter how good the mattress. Cleanse and bless your crystals and position them on arrival, and you will feel the difference immediately. As well as your quartz points, one small piece of rose quartz under the pillow will bring sweet dreams and peaceful sleep.

JET-LAG
Jet-lag is the price we pay for the speed and convenience of air travel and the symptoms increase on high-altitude, long-haul flights. Shifting time zones, altered magnetic fields,

culture and climate changes as well as exposure to radiation (radiation levels are greater on high-altitude flights and especially high at times of sun flares) germs, noise, chemicals and pesticides within the stuffy confines of an aircraft cabin, not surprisingly, take a high toll on body and mind. As a result you will almost certainly suffer from dehydration and you might expect any of the following symptoms: swollen feet, constipation and/or diarrhoea, dry eyes and skin, sore throat, headache, tiredness, irritability, disorientation, poor co-ordination, nausea, low blood sugar, anxiety, memory loss and irregular heartbeat.

You can take some practical measures to minimise your suffering. Swollen feet are the result of poor circulation from sitting for too long and this is compounded by low air pressure inside the aircraft. The best remedy is to move as much as possible — take a walk up and down the aisles if you can, but ankle rolling and stretching exercises are better than nothing — and be sure to travel in flat shoes that are slightly too big for you. Don't drink alcohol, tea or coffee, all of which will make you more dehydrated, but do drink lots and lots of good water — those extra trips to the loo are good exercise! Eat as little of the cooked, packaged or ready-prepared food as possible. Instead, choose fresh salads, fruit and juices. Ordering vegetarian or a special light diet at the time of booking can also be a good option.

Set your watch to the local time of your destination from the moment you take off, and when you arrive, spend time outdoors in daylight — exposure to natural daylight resets the body clock — and adjust your sleep patterns to local time as quickly as you can. An American friend of mine insists that you should eat some of the food straight away — especially those foods grown locally and in season — as another way of helping your system adapt to its new environment. If you are working, it is better to schedule important business for the evening if you have been flying east, and for the morning if you have been flying west, as your energy will be higher at these times.

CRYSTALS AND ESSENTIAL OILS

Crystals are very helpful when flying. Wear a good clean clear quartz, rainbow fluorite or aquamarine pendant to balance your energy field and keep you as clear as possible from the harmful pollutants and radiation in the aircraft. Mix up a remedy bottle containing a few drops of clear quartz or rainbow fluorite gem elixir combined with some Bach Flowers Rescue Remedy and add a few drops of the remedy to your drinking water during your flight. A second remedy containing rose quartz could be taken for twenty-four hours after landing. Alternatively, place a small piece of rose quartz under your pillow. Ideally, create a four square grid in your new bedroom with clear quartz points (see *Crystal travel kit*, above) to ensure peace and harmony.

As well as crystals in your hand luggage, essential oils are an invaluable support when travelling. They will lift your mood, relax you and keep your head and stomach clear. Lavender, camomile or geranium are all soothing and a few drops are good in an atomiser of pure water used as a rehydrating facial spray or sprinkled on a compress made from a cool, damp hand towel or handkerchief and applied to the wrists, throat, back of the neck and face. You can prepare a compress beforehand — about five drops of essential oil on a damp face cloth — and wrap it in a plastic bag. Ice cubes begged from the cabin crew and wrapped in a towel, which has been sprinkled with essential oils, also makes a very soothing compress to ease headaches.

When you reach your destination, revive yourself by placing your four travel quartz points at each corner of the bath ledge, points to the centre, and soaking in a reviving combination of lavender and grapefruit oil (two drops of each). Lavender will also discourage biting insects and, for those travelling rough, keep bed bugs at bay by sprinkling a few drops on the mattress or inside a sleeping bag.

TRAVEL SICKNESS
Travel sickness can be a problem, on land, sea or in the air, but peppermint and ginger oils are excellent for combating nausea and nervous stomachs. One drop in a cup of hot water just before you set off or a sugar cube smeared with a single drop of one of these oils will settle you or your children (a few sugar cubes are very easily carried in a plastic bag in your hand luggage). A few drops of eucalyptus, peppermint or lavender in a handkerchief will also ease nausea and weariness. Children will find carrying their own pocket crystal a comfort and support if they are nervous (see Chapter 9) and a remedy bottle made up with citrine gem elixir and Bach Flowers Rescue Remedy is a good settler. If you wish to sleep — a good idea on a long flight — hold a little piece of rose quartz in your 'receiving' hand (see page 52) and ask it to bring you peaceful sleep.

Cheerful adaptation to the new environment, a sense of humour and an open mind are the secrets of a happy traveller. Relax and remain flexible. Rather than trying to control what is beyond you — which will inevitably lead to tension and stress — you can be fairly certain that sometimes things will go awry and plans will need to change. By accepting change and the inevitable differences you will encounter with openness and wonder, each new experience will bring growth and the awareness that travel broadens the mind.

CHAPTER 11

The Workplace

The world is too much with us; late and soon,
Getting and spending, we lay waste our powers.

William Wordsworth

W e spend nearly a quarter of our entire lives at work, sometimes in an environment over which we have little control and among people with whom we do not necessarily have a natural affinity. While the vast majority work in large office blocks and factory units, work patterns are changing and more people now work from home. Although this may have distinct environmental benefits, it can also result in isolation and alienation as humans are sociable creatures and the stimulation we get from contact, and even conflict, has well-documented benefits to our health and well-being. But fortunately we are also adaptable, resourceful and creative, and crystals can be used to stimulate these qualities and improve our working lives, whatever the circumstances.

SICK BUILDINGS

In 1995 the Inland Revenue decided to demolish its 19 storey office in Bootle because 50 per cent of the 2,000 staff experienced frequent flu-like symptoms over a period of five years, which was thought to be caused by micro-organisms in the ventilation ducts. They were responding to a now well-established problem — sick building syndrome.

Sick building syndrome (SBS) has been defined by the World Health Organisation ('Indoor Air Quality Research',

EURO Reports and Studies, No. 103, 1986) as a new frequency of irritative symptoms from the eyes, nose, throat and lower airways, skin reactions, unspecific hypersensitivity reactions, mental fatigue, headache, nausea or dizziness while in a particular building. Research by the WHO suggested that as many as 30 per cent of new and reconditioned office blocks in developed countries display signs of SBS with 10 to 30 per cent of occupants affected.

In the early 1980s office workers were diagnosed with sickness resulting from SBS, caused by such pollutants as formaldehyde (from furniture and insulating materials), benzene (from paint) and the solvent trichloroethene, concentrated in air-conditioned buildings. Studies have found that it can cause a 40 per cent drop in productivity and a 30 per cent rise in absenteeism.

Sealed buildings, air conditioning, the use of synthetic building materials and the greatly increased use of electronic equipment have contributed to complaints of SBS as shown in a study of two buildings reported in *Safetyline* magazine (No.18, April 1993) for WorkSafe Western Australia. It showed that sick buildings are often the result of ventilation problems arising from inadequate planning. One, a new building, had high levels of formaldehyde and carbon dioxide, light glare and uncomfortably high temperatures as a direct result of poor planning, the use of materials emitting volatile chemicals and a lack of fresh air. The other, a twenty-year-old building, had poor air circulation and contained high levels of nitrogen dioxide and carbon monoxide due to poor office design and a badly positioned air intake.

These sorts of environmental problems in buildings can be prevented at the design stage, which include properly located air intakes, adjustable ventilation and the availability of natural light. Low chemical emission materials can be used in construction and furnishing and safer, less polluting cleaning products can be used inside the building.

PLANTS AND CRYSTALS FOR HEALTH

Work on improving the living conditions of astronauts showed that some of the causes of problems were easily and inexpensively removed by pot plants where an interaction is thought to take place between the plant and micro-organisms in its roots. Most useful are chrysanthemums which counteract benzene, English ivy and peace lilies which counteract trichloroethene, and the spider plant which offsets formaldehyde.

Along with healing plants, your workspace can be made more healthy with placements of quartz crystals to set up clean energy spaces that protect from harmful radiation as well as enhancing a healthy, balanced and positive mood.

CRYSTAL FREQUENCIES

So how do you continue to use computers, portable phones and other essential electronic equipment without suffering from the effects of background electrical radiation? As a basic rule of thumb, it is always a good idea to set up a protective grid for sacred space if at all practicable. (See page 39 for details of the four square grid.) You might set up the grid for the entire room, or just around your own workstation. Just because you can't see the radiation or the changes in your own energy field does not mean that changes do not take place all the time. But you can discover electromagnetic field disturbance with a hand-held compass (see page 37), which will give you some awareness of the reality of the energy soup we all live in. A quartz crystal placed in front of your computer monitor will transform any energy emissions, restoring them to a balance that is harmonious with your own energy.

HEALTH RISKS

There is no question that electronic developments such as portable phones have transformed our lives. Apart from the question of whether it is always a blessing to be so accessible, the electromagnetic energy emitted by the cellular phone is definitely incompatible with our own, much faster brain wave patterns. Exposure to high levels of electromagnetic radiation causes tissue damage and can produce other adverse effects such as altered behavioural responses, lens cataracts and risks to pregnancy. As yet there is no definitive evidence linking electromagnetic exposure, or indeed portable phones, with the development of tumours and cancer, but research is ongoing and the recommended safety levels of specific absorption rates and the time of exposure is under constant revue. Older people and young children are undoubtedly more sensitive, as are those who are already suffering from ill health and low energy.

The National Cancer Institute in the USA is currently undertaking major research into possible links between exposure to electromagnetic radiation and brain tumours, and previous NCI and NCI-funded epidemiological studies have already linked the increased risk of brain cancer with exposure to high doses of ionising radiation (such as X-rays and gamma rays which can cause chromosomal changes), occupational exposure to organic solvents and some pesticides, and employment in electrical and electronics-related jobs. Genetic factors and certain chemicals and DNA viruses can also cause brain tumours.

PORTABLE PHONES

What is certain is that less energy is absorbed when the phone is held away from the head, so it is far better to use a separate mouth and ear piece so that you don't have to hold the cell pressed up close to your brain. A client of mine keeps a small quartz point taped to his portable phone. Portable phones can certainly interfere with electrical equipment, including some pacemaker models when the phone antenna is within 20 cm (8 inches) of the pacemaker. Ventilators and powered wheelchairs may also be affected by some phones operating near these devices.

EFFECTS OF SOUND

Sound is another important environmental consideration that can shape and alter mood and health, depending on the level and frequency of exposure. Four different categories of brain wave rates have been equated to different states of consciousness. Measured in hertz (units of sound waves), they are:

1. beta waves (14–20 Hz) our normal waking consciousness;
2. alpha waves (8–13 Hz) daydreaming and meditative state;
3. theta waves (4–7 Hz) deep meditation, trance and sleep;
4. delta waves (0.5–3 Hz) deep sleep and very profound healing and meditational states.

Certain sounds can definitely change brain wave patterns and have a strong influence on your health and well-being.

It is an old chestnut, often quoted, that listening to specific musical forms such as baroque music will produce wave patterns in the brain which are relaxing and facilitate high levels of learning ability, while more discordant sounds create disharmony and poor concentration. The deliberate manipulation of brainwaves through sound, known as entrainment, is found in every cultural tradition that uses sound, from Gregorian chant to Hindu mantras and shamanic drumming, and it is the same principle used by sound healers. Noise is a fact of modern life, from machinery and traffic to the inevitable 'muzak' so common in public spaces, and our energy can be debilitated by the cacophony around us.

According to Dr Alfred Tomatis, a French physician who has made the effects of sound on the human ear his life study, there are two kinds of sound — one that is tiring to listen to and another that is healing. He found that sounds containing high frequency harmonics were most beneficial and that frequencies around 8,000 Hz could charge the central nervous system and the brain cortex. Benedictine monks, who gave up their regular six to eight hours of daily chanting after a new abbot decided it was a waste of time, were soon suffering from depression and extreme tiredness. After various attempted cures, with no improvement, Dr Tomatis was consulted and, isolating the absence of chanting as the sole change in their ages-old routine, suggested they reinstate their daily chanting. The monks soon returned to full health and were able to get back to their long rigorous days of prayer and labour.

The same property of quartz crystals that transforms one form of energy — pressure into electricity, for example — also operates in relation to sound. Crystallo-luminescence is the term used when crystals convert sound vibrations into light, through compressing and pulsing the energy to move it from a lower form of energy (sound) to the higher level of energy (light). Quartz crystals transmit healing frequencies when used with chanting (see Chapter 20) and they can strengthen your energy field by transforming harmful frequencies. It is also a very good idea to protect yourself with a gem elixir that will strengthen your resistance (as described in Chapter 6). If possible, introduce some positive sounds into your workspace — a little Mozart, perhaps, a recording of Gregorian or Tibetan chants, *feng shui* wind chimes or bells tuned to a healing note above a doorway or beside an open window. The sound of running water from an indoor fountain is very soothing and has the additional benefits of looking delightful and emitting health-giving negative ions.

ENERGY VAMPIRES

You are probably aware that some people seem to make you tired while others leave you feeling on top of the world. These are unconscious energy vampires and boosters. A key insight in James Redfield's *The Celestine Prophesy* is that we are all in unconscious energetic competition. Whether you are radiating energy or leeching it may depend on factors such as how much attention you are giving or getting, your general health level, your emotional happiness, and your exposure to and appreciation of beauty.

What is certain is that until we become more conscious and work to balance this debilitating see-saw, we are all suffering and living well below our potential. By seeking to steal energy from one another, we temporarily take control of the other person, so conflicts are, ultimately, all about stealing energy, whatever the expressed reason. When you pay close attention to someone, you give them energy and thus energy virtually equates with attention in human transactions. In order to steal energy or get attention, we have developed from childhood a variety of control dramas or 'games' (as Dr Eric Berne described them in *Games People Play*). Once you gain insight into your own dramas, you can begin to make conscious choices and changes. An awareness of beauty, allied to an opening up, permits you to draw energy directly from the cosmos, thus obviating the need to steal from other people. The ultimate opening up is the mystical experience of unity. You can obtain energy from the cosmos by focusing on its beauty, allowing yourself to feel close, then breathing it in. A beautiful amethyst crystal bed or clear quartz cluster placed on your desk acts as a constant focus of beauty as well as bringing a radiant balanced energy to your environment. Wear a crystal pendant or carry a crystal on your body in a little pouch as a constant protection if you feel that you are particularly susceptible to being drained by fellow workers or are in a job where you are constantly dealing with different people and are subject to lots of demands on your energy. Clear and smoky quartz, amethyst or citrine might all be good choices.

NATURAL LIGHT AND SAD

Another factor that affects us all is the availability and quality of light and, as most of us spend the majority of our adult waking life at work, this is a factor that needs particular attention in the workplace. Animals react to the changing seasons with changes in mood and behaviour, and human beings are no exception. While most people find they eat and sleep slightly more in winter and dislike the dark mornings and short days, some suffer symptoms which cause real distress. This is known as Seasonal Affective Disorder (SAD), sometimes called winter depression or the winter blues.

Symptoms tend to start as early as September each year
and last through until April, but are at their worst in the
darkest months and might include:

• extreme fatigue and lack of energy
• sleep problems such as oversleeping but not refreshed
• overeating and carbohydrate craving, leading to
  overweight
• depression, despair, misery, guilt, anxiety, frustration
  and a sense of hopelessness, family problems, avoiding company, irritability, loss of libido, loss of feeling
• lethargy — everything an effort
• physical symptoms such as joint pain or stomach
  problems, lowered resistance to infection as well as
  behavioural problems, especially in young people

The problem apparently stems from the lack of bright light in
winter. SAD is more common in northern countries (north of
the equator) because the winter day gets shorter as you go
further north. According to research, less than one per cent
of the population of Florida have SAD, while in Alaska as
many as 10 per cent may suffer. Similar statistics relate to
northern Europe where up to 10 per cent of people put up
with some of the milder symptoms. Incidence increases with
distance from the equator except where there is snow on the
ground which increases the light reflection. More women,
children and adolescents are diagnosed, so good light quality
is of great importance in schools.

It is known that the nerve centres in our brains
controlling our daily rhythms and moods are stimulated by
the amount of light entering the eyes. During the night the
pineal gland produces a substance called melatonin which

makes us drowsy. At daybreak the bright light causes the gland to stop producing this melatonin. But on dull winter days, especially indoors, not enough light is received to trigger this waking up process.

It is possible that the 'biological clock' in the brain regulating hormones, sleep and mood, may run more slowly in the winter for people susceptible to SAD. Other theories suggest that SAD is due to imbalances in brain chemistry, particularly serotonin and dopamine, or even due to a reduced retinal light sensitivity in the winter. Whatever the cause, bright light is beneficial to those suffering from SAD and research has shown that light can stimulate and restore normal brain and hormone function.

Using a light box every day is helpful in treating SAD, as is a winter holiday in a brightly lit climate — whether it be skiing or somewhere hot. The ideal level of light is about as bright as a spring morning on a clear day. It is not necessary to stare at the light — just as long as the light reaches the eyes. 2,500 lux (lux is the technical measure of brightness) is about the level needed, which is approximately five times brighter than a well-lit office, while a normal living-room might be as low as 100 lux. Brighter lights, up to 10,000 lux, will be even more effective. While changing to special daylight, colour matching or full spectrum light bulbs will not produce the *amount* of light needed to counteract SAD, the provision of these healthier forms of artificial light does ease eye strain and beneficially affects mood. Selenite is known to be helpful in cases of light sensitivity. Try placing a piece of this pure, translucent white crystal within your aura for clarity and strength.

Crystals not only reflect light but also transmit a greater range of the light spectrum than glass, making them ideal for high-precision lenses and optical equipment. Take advantage of these qualities to bring balanced light frequencies into your workspace. The radiance of a sparkling clear quartz cluster will increase your energy as well as enhancing the quality of light available to you. If you suspect you suffer from SAD, try wearing a clear quartz pendant for its balanced energy and light and seek the advice of your doctor for possible referral to a light therapy specialist.

INSOMNIA AND SHIFT WORK

There is now well-documented research to show that scheduled exposure to full spectrum bright light at night and darkness during the day will help with insomnia caused by shift working. The use of crystals will also help to regulate the body clock and assist in adapting more easily to new work and sleep patterns. I would recommend carrying a well-cleansed clear quartz on the body during a night shift and that a rose quartz be placed under the pillow to encourage peaceful daytime sleep.

CHAPTER 12

Concentration and Inspiration

The truth dazzles gradually, or else the world would be blind.

Emily Dickinson

There are aspects of work that call for specific energies and talents. Studying and planning demand concentration, focus and clarity of thought, whereas the key to creative work is inspiration combined with the drive and skill with which to express it. Success in all these ventures comes from a real confidence founded on a clear connection with the flow of life. Crystals help in ways that will make a real difference to your work.

TRUST IN LIFE

Donne said 'no man is an island', yet due to sadness, fear and lack of love, many people live as if this were the case, cutting themselves off from the source of joy and abundance which is within them and all around them. Sadly few are given the life-affirming nourishment and sense of selfhood in early childhood that enables us to trust in life. I do not claim that crystals will make up for experiences of fear and shame but, by aligning with their spiritual clarity and their deep earthy wisdom, we can find a pathway to peace and harmony that may help to bring a deeper sense of the unity of all life. When we do not have peace and confidence in ourselves, we do not have peace and trust in our lives and depend more and more on the fickle opinions of others (who are often lost and afraid themselves) for our sense of worth.

Whatever your gifts — and you do indeed possess unique life-enhancing gifts — bringing your energy system into alignment will help you to access your wider potential and the sense of being that simply makes your heart sing. You don't need to be a brain surgeon, a rocket scientist or a prima ballerina to be a wonderful human being. Indeed, you cannot get a degree in the art of living and many amazing people live generous, loving and peaceful lives without it ever reaching the newspapers. Yet it is these souls who are healing the world through kindness, fostering good relationships, and through being most truly themselves.

Many years ago in London I travelled to work by bus and counted myself lucky if I caught the bus with the special conductor. Over the years I watched this gentle man bring healing to all who travelled his route, with a kind word here, a helping hand there, or the warmth of a smile. And, like ripples in a pool, he sent his passengers on their way to spread the good will. I have no idea whether he was conscious of what he was doing, but he brought to his work a natural grace and generosity that had the power to transform pain and sadness into hope and love. And what an efficient choice of job for a healer! He touched the lives of hundreds of people every day.

CREATING HARMONY

To find and maintain your own centre, it is helpful to do something that makes you conscious of your life, the way you use and express your energy and your connection with the life force. Balancing your *chakras* is an ideal way to do this and regular practice will bring untold benefits in terms of your focus and creativity as well as bringing a greater sense of meaning to all that you do. I recommend you pre-record this exercise and allow about twenty minutes in a quiet place. My enduring thanks go to Glen Park from whose book, *The Art of Changing*, I took the basis for this exercise, and much invaluable wisdom besides.

Take a clear quartz crystal in your receiving hand and touch each centre with the crystal as you move through the visualisation. This is an ideal way to start each day.

Exercise: Chakra Balance
Sit comfortably, with your spine straight and your feet flat on the ground.

Close your eyes and allow your breathing to come naturally and easily.

Your neck should be long at the back and your chin tucked in slightly so that your head is well supported.

Bring your attention to the base of the spine.

Imagine a strong, clear red light at your coccyx spiralling outwards filling your pelvis and travelling right down your legs to your feet and toes.

Think of a rich red sunset or the heart of a deep ruby crystal.

As you visualise the strength and energy of red, sense your connection with the earth and imagine that roots extend through the soles of your feet deep into Mother Earth nourishing and supporting you.

Now say to yourself:

'I accept my instinctual nature, the part of me which is purely animal.'

Then draw your attention and the energy up to your sacrum a little below your navel and imagine a soft orange light spreading out to fill your lower abdomen, warm and comforting like the glow of firelight as you say:

'I accept my emotional nature, my need for pleasure and nurturing' and feel the warmth and energy spread right across your belly.

Then bring the energy and your awareness up to your solar plexus.

Imagine a golden yellow light, strong and clear like the sun, filling the whole of your upper abdomen as you say: 'I accept my power, my ability to succeed and my need to have some control over my life.'

And picture the sun as a shield of protection as well as a source of great strength and power.

Now bring this light up to your heart centre, the place of peace.

In the centre of your chest, level with your physical heart, imagine the light expressed as a clear, sunlit green.

Think of sunlight through fresh new leaves, the green of new life, growth and healing spreading across your chest and right down your arms to your fingertips.

This is the centre for unconditional love and acceptance of yourself and others, of all life, freely and without judgment as you say:

'I accept myself totally, exactly as I am now. I am.'

Next, bring the energy and attention up to your throat.

Imagine a clear, fresh sky blue light filling your throat and extending to the tips of your ears, your nose, your mouth and jaw as you say:

'I accept the way I express myself in the world.

I accept my creative nature.'

And sense the openness and flow at your throat.

Now bring your attention up to your brow.

Between your eyebrows see a deep indigo blue light like the night sky.

Fill out the rest of your head, like deep space as you say:
'I accept my wisdom, my understanding of reality'
and acknowledge the power of your own deep mind.
Finally draw the light up to the crown of your head.
Imagine a clear violet light streaming out from the top of
your head and dissolving into pure white light as you say:
'I accept my divinity, my connection with cosmic,
universal energy.'
Finally, imagine pure white light pouring down all around
you like a sparkling shower or waterfall, radiant energy
streaming through your energy field, your aura dissolving
away all that is outworn, limiting and painful as easily and
naturally as the mist dissolves in the morning.
And see the light fill you through the crown of your head.
Breathe it into the centre of your being on your in-breath
and, on your out-breath, imagine you are sending the light
to every cell and atom of your body.
See the whole of you, inside and out, radiant with the
light, filled and surrounded by the life force energy as you
say:
'I am in the light and the light is in me.'

Continue to breathe quietly and circulate the light for a
few minutes.

STUDYING
When you need to study or are working in an area that
demands intense concentration, it is particularly important
that you set yourself a timetable of regular breaks, including
fresh air, good breathing, food, exercise and relaxation. You
might consider alternating your breaks so that one is a short
walk in the fresh air, the next a food break, the next a gentle

relaxation or meditation exercise, and so on. The breathing and relaxation techniques in Chapter 17 will provide you with a framework of support — you might try either *Love and Bless your Body* or *Remembering* — simple exercises designed to extend your awareness of the moment.

Amethyst is famous for creating an atmosphere of focus and concentration, as well as bringing protection to your energy field. Ideally, place an amethyst bed on your desk or wear an amethyst pendant. Enhance brain function by carrying fluorite and use the energy amplification of calcite to facilitate learning and improve memory. If you are attracted to polished stones, beneficial forms are the pyramid and the obelisk, both of which will concentrate energy. A crystal cut into one of these forms could well be placed on your desk. Grids for the room or around your workspace that bring focus are either the universally useful four square grid or the double square mandala, made with eight crystals (see page 45).

SUCCESS AND PROSPERITY

It is good to bear in mind that if you nourish body, mind and spirit with generosity towards yourself and others, it will attract prosperity. It is important to keep the energy, whether it be in the form of cash or well-being, flowing freely at all times. The saying that nothing attracts success like success is true. Do not be tempted to hoard your treasures and gifts — material or spiritual — if you want them to increase. Give generously and you will receive likewise. Maintaining this energy flow lies at the heart of the ever pragmatic practice of *feng shui*.

Sapphire is famously a stone of prosperity and it is said to make your dreams come true. The star sapphire, with its regular star-shaped radiance (caused by tiny cylindrical cavities within the stone that are parallel to the prism planes), is believed to be especially lucky. Green tourmaline also attracts great success and abundance. Wear either of these stones in a ring to maximise their influence. One of the most popular and readily available crystals associated with luck and prosperity is citrine, a golden form of quartz. Simply place or carry a little piece wherever you want to attract abundance — in your wallet, on your desk or by the telephone.

Citrine and the other golden stones, such as topaz and tiger eye, are also helpful in increasing your self-confidence and maintaining self-belief and self-reliance. Work too with the *Chakra balance* exercise above, paying specific attention to strengthening and protecting your third *chakra* at the solar plexus.

CREATIVITY

Creativity can be helped greatly by using crystals. A triangular grid of three quartz crystals (described in detail in Chapter 5) can amplify both the inspiration and the ability to express it that is so vital to creative work. For composing, design, writing or painting, a triangular grid will work wonders. Maintaining a high degree of energy through conscious connection with universal or divine energy via the crown *chakra*, and with Mother Earth via the base, is especially vital for creative people, as the act of creating burns a great deal of vital force which needs constant replenishing. Again I would recommend the *Chakra balance* as a daily exercise, including circulating the light through the aura for clarity and strength. *Treading the light* (in Chapter 19) is another excellent way of maintaining a good energy flow.

MUSIC AND THE ARTS

Celestite brings special gifts to those working with music and the creative arts. It allows creative energy to move with airy freedom, delicacy and refinement and facilitates the expression of inner vision and inspiration. A manifestation quartz crystal — one that completely encloses a smaller crystal inside — is a rare but perfect channel for creative energy. Tiger iron, which combines gold tiger eye, jasper and hematite, is also wonderful for encouraging creative excellence. Rose quartz, one of the most universally delightful and helpful of crystals, will enhance your receptivity to all forms of beauty, art and music, as well as stimulating the imagination and bringing you its love, encouragement and protection.

Crystals in the Garden

I believe a blade of grass is no less than the
journey-work of the stars
Walt Whitman

Crystals are really in their element in the garden. As blossoms from the earth, they bring a special beauty and light that will add an extra dimension to any garden — be it a modest balcony or roof space, a productive vegetable plot, a lively family garden or your own quiet corner of paradise. Even if you do not have a garden of your own, you may have some community space — at school or near your home — where the authorities might be open to small creative projects that would be fun for everyone. This section offers many such ideas as well as practical ways crystals can be used to benefit the plants themselves and the people that grow with them.

CHAPTER 13

Crystal Gardening

If nature is your teacher, your soul will awaken.
Johann Wolfgang von Goethe

You can apply your knowledge of the way crystals work to help you in the garden. By acknowledging the reality of energy fields and the interplay of natural forces, you can use crystals as part of an overall approach that will help maintain optimum balance in the ecology of the garden. It is important, however, that you do not expect crystals to do all the work — you would not give up food, drink and rest relying solely on crystals for your well-being. Crystals are just one helpful tool for healthy living. For a really blooming garden of happy plants, you need to attend to their health and nutrition, their environment, their compatibility with their neighbours and the influence of natural forces.

One of the greatest exponents of a practical (and very effective) system of agriculture and gardening founded on spiritual principles was the teacher and philosopher Rudolph Steiner. As part of his work (known as anthroposophy), Steiner developed biodynamics, an approach to gardening and agriculture that integrates careful observation of natural phenomena with thought and spiritual knowledge. It is a science of life forces which recognises the basic principles at work in nature and approaches agriculture by incorporating these principles to bring about balance and healing. The study and practice of biodynamics honours the earth as a living being, and describes an evolution of the constitution of humanity and the kingdoms of nature which, for serious gardeners, is a rewarding and continuously evolving path.

Biodynamic Gardening

Biodynamic gardening takes into account the widest spectrum influencing plant growth from the depths of the earth to the heights of the heavens and acknowledges that everything in nature reveals something of its essence by its form. Therefore careful observations of nature — in shade and full sun, in wet and dry areas, on different soils — will give you a more fluid grasp of the elements and their effects, and as you learn to read the language of nature you can become creative, bringing new emphasis and balance through your specific actions. In this way practitioners and experimenters over the last seventy years have added tremendously to Steiner's original work in this field.

Planetary influences

In Steiner's view planetary influences are of key significance to the well-being of plants. The light of the sun, moon, planets and stars reaches the plants in regular rhythms. Each contributes to the life, growth and form of the plant. By understanding the effect of each rhythm, you can time your ground preparation, sowing, cultivating and harvesting to the advantage of the crops you grow. For example, it is best to sow between days 1 and 7 after the New Moon, and to harvest at the Full Moon when the produce will keep and store better.

Biodynamics recognises that soil itself can be alive, and this vitality supports and affects the quality of the plants that grow in it and subsequently the value of the food we eat. Therefore, one of the fundamentals of biodynamics is to build up stable humus in the soil through composting. We gain our physical strength from the process of breaking down the food we eat. The more vital our food, the more it stimulates our own activity. So biodynamic farmers and gardeners aim primarily for quality rather than quantity. Chemical agriculture has developed short cuts that give greater yields by adding soluble minerals to the soil which the plants take up via water, by-passing their natural ability to seek from the soil what they need for health, vitality and growth. This ultimately results in deadened soil and artificially stimulated growth.

BIODYNAMIC PREPARATIONS

Biodynamically produced food undoubtedly grows with a strong connection to healthy, living soil. Composting is a key activity in biodynamic gardening and Steiner developed what are known as Biodynamic Preparations, replacing instinctive wisdom and superstition with his new science of cosmic influences. Naturally occurring plant and animal materials are combined in specific recipes in certain seasons of the year and then placed in compost piles. These preparations carry concentrated forces within them and are used to organise the random recycled waste elements within the compost piles. When the process is complete, the resulting preparations are medicines for the earth which are believed to draw life forces from the cosmos. One of the preparations is used on the earth before planting to stimulate soil life, and one is sprayed on to the leaves of growing plants to enhance their capacity to receive the light.

Whether or not you want to go biodynamic in your garden, it is certainly beneficial to be as organic as possible so that the integrity of the garden's ecology is maintained, albeit with plenty of weeding! Certainly you will reap the rewards in delicious and wholesome fruits and vegetables, and by

attracting a wide range of birds, butterflies and other
creatures to share your corner of paradise.

COMPANION PLANTING

There are certain plants that are particularly compatible
when planted together. This companion planting has various
benefits, the main one being the suppression of pests and
diseases. Some notable examples include:

Apple trees
Chives growing at the roots of apple trees can help to
counteract scab. Nasturtiums planted close by will repel
woolly aphids. Harvested apples and potatoes should not be
stored in the same place as they will not keep well and lose
flavour.

Asparagus
Asparagus and tomatoes benefit each other and should be
planted close where possible — something called asparagin
in the asparagus helps control some of the soil pests which
affect tomatoes. Parsley also helps asparagus.

Beans
Beans add nitrogen to the soil and so are good grown in a
mixed border. They thrive close to carrots and cauliflower,
they will help cucumbers and cabbages and they do well
planted near beets. However, they tend to inhibit the growth
of onions, garlic and shallots. Broad beans and potatoes do
well when interplanted, keeping insect pests down. Bush
beans and strawberries are also said to be mutually beneficial.

Borage
Strawberries benefit from borage near by. It will attract honey
bees. Borage can become rampant in the garden but it can be
made into a very useful liquid manure by filling a black refuse

sack with cut stems and leaving them to decompose (best left inside a waterproof container). The resulting strong black liquid should be diluted in water (5 per cent per volume) as needed and either watered into the soil or sprayed on already well-established plants.

Elderberry
Grown near the compost heap, they will assist fermentation. Elders make very light and fluffy humus around their roots, which is excellent added to topsoil in the garden.

Foxglove
Gives strength and endurance as well as stimulating the growth of plants in its vicinity.

French marigolds
French marigolds (*Tagetes patula*) excrete a substance from their roots which kills soil nematodes, tiny worms which are particularly damaging to rose gardens. They control potato nematodes in the same way and are very useful in greenhouses for controlling white fly.

Hyssop
Planted near grapevines, they will increase the yield and lure cabbage white butterflies away from cabbages.

Lemon balm
Radiates a generally helpful atmosphere to the plants around it. A beehive rubbed on the inside with a handful of lemon balm will always keep the swarm in that hive.

Mint
Spearmint and other mints repel black fly beetles, cabbage butterfly caterpillars and ants (therefore probably helping to control aphids). Indoors mint will repel clothes moths.

Nasturtiums
Nasturtiums planted in the greenhouse and with tomatoes will greatly reduce white fly. Grown near radishes, they

enhance the flavour and texture. They will keep broccoli free of aphids and, planted under apple trees, keep woolly aphids at bay. A good spray can be made from nasturtium by placing the cut plant covered with water in a saucepan and heating to just boiling point. Remove from heat and dilute the infusion with four parts water. Stir for about ten minutes while the liquid cools. Use the spray immediately as a pest control for plants and trees.

Oak
Oak leaf mulch repels slugs, cutworms and maybug grubs. Oak trees have the special ability to accumulate lots of calcium in their bark and so preparations made from oak bark can be beneficial where plants are calcium deficient.

Onions
Alternating a row of onions with a row of carrots has the benefit of repelling both onion fly and carrot fly. Camomile helps onions to thrive — plant one camomile plant to every 4 metres of onion row.

Parsley
Parsley attracts honey bees and helps both roses and tomatoes.

Potatoes
Grow well with peas, beans, sweetcorn and cabbage. Plant with alternating double rows of peas as potatoes like the nitrogen they get from the pea roots. Horseradish plants at the corners of the potato plot will also keep potatoes healthy. Hemp grown near potatoes is said to prevent late blight.

Rosemary
Repels carrot fly in the vegetable plot and is a good companion with sage.

Roses
Roses and garlic are famous companion plants and in Bulgaria garlic and onions are interplanted with roses, where

it is found that the roses produce a stronger perfume as a result. Roses and parsley are another winning combination. Do not plant roses close to box as the spreading roots of the box interfere with the roots of the roses — deep-rooted companions are better than spreading rooted ones.

Rue

Repels houseflies and horseflies and, grown in window boxes, will prevent flies coming into the house where this is a problem — maybe near the kitchen.

Sage

Sage and rosemary are good companions. Grown among cabbages, sage discourages cabbage butterfly and even strewing twigs of sage will repel this pest. Sage planted beside cabbage will also make the cabbage more tender and digestible and is generally good in the vegetable garden.

Spearmint

Repels rodents and ants, helping to control aphids which are placed on plants by the ants.

Stinging nettles

Stinging nettles are very helpful in the garden in several ways. When planted near by, they will stop fruit and vegetables spoiling (especially tomatoes) and they change the chemistry of companion plants, bringing greater potency and increasing the quantity of essential oil produced by the plants. Nettles also stimulate the production of humus in the soil and they will stimulate a healthy fermentation in the compost heap. To make a liquid nettle manure, cover the cut stems with water and leave to decompose for three weeks. After three weeks use as a general spray on plants for greater strength, health and resistance — add clear quartz crystal water for increased potency (see *Crystal waters* below).

Strawberries
Strawberries particularly like borage as companions but also do well beside lettuces, spinach and dwarf beans.

Tansy
Tansy repels ants and flies and is good planted by a peach tree or other soft fruit where flies are a pest. A good addition to the compost heap as it concentrates potassium.

Valerian
Valerian helps most vegetables because it stimulates phosphorus activity in its vicinity. It attracts earth worms and the juice can be made into a spray which, if used once a month in summer, will encourage general health and resistance in all your plants.

Yarrow
Yarrow planted with aromatic herbs will enhance their aroma and increase the potency of medicinal herbs. Small quantities of yarrow in the vegetable plot will increase resistance to disease. Yarrow enriches the nutritional value of pasture for cattle.

This is just a sample of helpful plant alliances. For more, see the Bibliography for further reading.

COMPANION CRYSTALS
Different crystals can be seen to broadly assist plants but will have a more generally strengthening effect on the energy field of the plants and of the soil in general than in the specific types of symbiosis described above. But there are exceptions: roses really do enjoy the presence of rose quartz; citrine enhances and is brightened by marigolds, sunflowers and yellow daisies; and all plants are supported by the presence of moss agate and clear quartz. For specific

properties of different crystals, see the Colour Crystal Directory at the end of the book.

One of the most effective ways of distributing crystal energy in the garden is through the use of crystal waters as plant sprays and by watering into the soil. When preparing a new bed for planting, you can spray the freshly cultivated soil with a clear quartz water to bring light and energy to the soil. Leave at least twenty-four hours before planting which should ideally be during the week following the new moon.

CRYSTAL WATERS

Crystal and gem waters should be made in the way described in Chapter 6. Elixirs should not be used on plants except in very diluted quantities, as the alcohol will not benefit the plants and could scorch tender leaves. Keeping a quartz crystal in your watering can is a good way of making sure you are using high energy water on your plants. Add clear quartz water to your compost heap and to your liquid manures (see *Companion planting* above) for extra vitality.

CRYSTAL GRIDS

To create a clear and energised plot for planting vegetables, you might like to consider creating a crystal grid in the soil by sinking a quartz point at each corner of the plot, points directed to the centre of the plot. Alternatively, you might plant a crystal at either end of a row of vegetables to activate and energise the whole row. Where you have a plant that needs to form strong roots and to get off to a really good start, you might plant a crystal in the roots of the plant at the time of planting — moss agate, rose quartz or clear quartz are good choices.

The plants in your greenhouse will also benefit from the placement of a crystal grid to maintain a balanced energy field within which they can grow. This is especially helpful if your greenhouse is heated and includes electrical wiring, propagators and other electrical equipment. The basic four square grid is probably the most useful. You can use four medium-sized quartz points as described in Chapter 5 or four equal-sized lumps of rose quartz.

AILING PLANTS
To counteract the increasing effects of pollution, crystals can be used to strengthen plants and help them to adapt to harsher conditions. As I have described in previous chapters, it is important to clear any imbalance or disease before applying more energy to the energy field — whether it belongs to a person or a plant. The presence of individual crystals tends to be stimulating and you should bear this in mind when considering the specific influences you wish to bring to your plants.

As a general rule, it is best to clear damaging conditions affecting the plant as best you can before stimulating the energy field of the plant. A weakened plant can first be cleared by making a clearing grid around the plant (to clear or draw off negative conditions the quartz points should be directed away from the plant) and a little while later the plant can be stimulated and strengthened (even more effective with a waxing moon) by turning the points of the grid to face inwards towards the plant (thus becoming an energising grid) and placing a little crystal close to the stem of the plant (within its energy field to attract more energy to the plant).

CHAPTER 14

Gardens to Refresh the Spirit

One is nearer God's heart in a garden
Than anywhere else on earth.

Dorothy Frances Gurney

Crystals can be incorporated into the garden in a variety of ways to create and enhance specific atmospheres. Outdoor spaces, even very small ones, can provide a haven of quiet contemplation or a playful, fantasy setting for imaginative adults or children. The garden is an ideal environment for consciously creating a meditation space and one of the most perfect of these is the classic Japanese Zen garden described below. If you let your imagination guide you, you will find lots of ways of adapting traditional forms, or devising entirely new ones, with the help of crystals and special stones.

A ZEN GARDEN

The harmonious placement of each plant, stone and feature probably reaches its ultimate expression in the Zen Buddhist gardens of Japan. The Zen garden is an idealisation of nature, a created paradise where, unlike so many Western gardens, every aspect of the environment is seen in relationship to and as symbolic of the balanced forces of the universe. Elements of space and form, scale and texture, light and shade, stillness and movement, seen in the natural landscape and expressing the primary opposing forces of either *yin* or *yang*, are re-created in a meticulously balanced ideal.

The earliest Japanese gardens were entirely influenced by the Chinese, very stylised and usually laid out to the south of the house. A pond with an island was the central feature with, at the north end of the pond, a waterfall that tumbled down an artificial hill. By the Kamakura period (1192–1333) two main types of gardens had developed — hill or flat — depending on the site. Mount Fuji, the mountain of ideal form, became the main inspiration for the hill garden, made of hills and ponds, while the flat garden was intended to represent a stretch of water with its shores and islands. Although very small in scale, the intention was always to express the spirit of the landscape and this scaling down of landscapes reached its ultimate expression in bonsai gardening where even small trays might contain complete miniature gardens.

To create and appreciate the Japanese garden requires an awareness of the symbolism of each element and its relation to the whole. The most famous example of an abstract garden is the Ryoan-ji in Kyoto, an enclosed rectangular area covered with raked sand in which are set 15 stones divided into five groups of three. While these stones may represent rocky outcrops in the sea, it is essentially the harmony of its relationships that makes this garden so satisfying.

In Buddhist Zen gardens, nine stones, four recumbent and five standing, were used to symbolise the nine spirits of the Buddhist pantheon, and even in the secular Japanese garden it was thought to be unlucky not to include the three sacred stones — the 'Guardian Stone', the 'Stone of Adoration' and the 'Stone of the Two Deities' (or the 'Stone of Completeness') — and all the stones acquired names suggested by their shape and use, such as the 'Recumbent Ox Stone' or the 'Seagull-resting Stone'. But beyond what they represented, stones were a vital part of an aesthetic plan and had to be placed in ways that appeared natural and harmonious.

Sacred gardens were developed as a focus for prolonged contemplation by the monks and the modern Zen garden still relies on three main elements — plants, water and rocks — the stones being the main feature. Each stone is chosen for its individual size, shape, colour and texture and arranged according to the 'principle of three forces', from the use in Chinese painting of vertical, horizontal and diagonal lines to represent the heavens, the earth and humanity. The vertical lines, symbolising the heavens, provide depth; the horizontal lines (the earth) give stability; and the diagonals, humanity, are seen as the bridge providing a comfortable transition between heaven and earth.

MAKING YOUR OWN ZEN GARDEN

You can create your own Zen garden by considering some basic guidelines and then making careful use of your chosen elements and their relationships. It is usually a good idea to keep your design as simple as possible, taking time to choose each of your elements carefully, conscious of what they mean to you and what their placement might signify. For example a particular stone might represent a high point or event in your life; two stones standing together or a group of stones might signify a special relationship or your family.

While the specific use of crystals is not traditional in Zen gardens, the beauty of this form can be enhanced by the intuitive addition of rose, clear, smoky or white quartz stones or pebbles along a pathway, perhaps, or surrounding a pool. Some white gravels, as well as having a high quartz content, contain a high degree of sparking mica which will bring specific qualities of energy and light. Raked sand or gravel is a substitute for water and rarely used in a garden where there is a real pond or stream, where the use of large stones and a more naturalistic setting often works better.

THE SPACE

Aspect — As already mentioned, the traditional setting of a Japanese garden lies to the south of the dwelling. Obviously this is not always practicable, but shelter is important and it is a good idea to screen your chosen area with walls or fencing, leaving gaps for glimpses of a distant view, if you have one. When planning your layout think particularly of what you will see from both the entrance to the garden and from the vantage point of a seat or summer house. A pathway (see *Paving stones* below) should wind slowly and irregularly between the two.

Soil — It is always advisable to check your soil type before planting anything new as each plant favours particular conditions. Rhododendrons, camellias and many magnolias — any of which would look well in a Japanese garden — need an acid soil in which to flourish. If you are laying concrete under gravel, you will need to consider drainage as damp ground or very heavy clay soil might present real problems. A small pond can often be helpful as well as being a delightful feature in its own right.

Natural features — Unless you have a fairly flat and uncluttered site, the classic raked gravel or sand garden may not work as it is supposed to represent a calm stretch of water. Also, if you have playful pets, the gravel may quickly take on the appearance of chaos as they are not easily persuaded to stick to pathways. In either case mosses, herbs or creeping plants (see *Plants* below) might be a better choice. If you do have a flat space and pets, cobbles or large flat stones (like those found in a riverbed or on the beach) are a better option than finer gravel.

Buildings and seats — As this type of garden is made for contemplation, remember to place a seat or seats in suitable places. In a traditional Japanese garden a teahouse might have overlooked the garden. You may already have a window, porch or summer house from which to view your Zen garden, but otherwise a simple covered seat or arbour is very welcome on cold or wet days.

STONES

I am grateful to Roni Jay's lovely book, *Sacred Gardens*, for much of the following information about the stones used in a Zen garden. She quotes the *Sakuteiki*, an eleventh-century gardening text, which states: 'For each stone there must be a supporting stone, for each upward-looking stone, a downward-looking stone, for each upright stone, a horizontal stone.'

Vertical stones — Vertical stones are of two types — the statue stone, the tallest used in a Zen garden, should have a conical top and a bulge in the middle. The second is the lower vertical stone which, while taller than it is wide, is shorter than the statue stone. Vertical stones which are laid flat are considered 'dead' and bring bad luck.

Horizontal stones — The flat stone (any irregular flat stone that is higher than a stepping stone), the arching stone (a stone of medium height that arches over to one side at the top), the recumbent ox stone (a long stone higher at one end, suggesting a resting animal). The latter two could be seen as diagonal or transitional stones.

Gravel/sand — Lay a layer of impermeable sheeting or concrete beneath the area you intend to gravel to prevent weeds coming up. You can choose from a wide range of colours, sizes and textures of stones. Coarse white sand can also be very effective. Raking the sand or gravel with a special wide-toothed rake in formal patterns to simulate water can look marvellous in a dry garden. The act of raking can be treated as a meditation in itself.

Paving stones — Large irregular flat stones of sandstone, granite, slate etc. laid to make comfortable steps across your lawn, gravel or ground cover. Traditionally paths are winding, allowing a meditative meander through the garden to the teahouse or sitting place. Stepping stones are used to deliberately slow the approach to the teahouse and while irregular, their arrangement is carefully planned. If the effect is not harmonious, smaller 'throwaway' stones, which are never stepped on, are used to redress the balance. Stepping stones are also used to create pathways and crossings in water gardens and just as much care should be taken in the choice of these stones as with others in the garden.

It is believed that you should listen to the spirit of the stone and let it guide you as to its appropriate location to avoid any possible bad luck.

WATER
Pools — It is beyond the scope of this book to give details of the creation of all but the simplest pool (see *A dark mirror*, pp 149). However, if you have a suitable space, a pool makes

a beautiful focus for a Zen garden. A formal carp-filled pool is traditional, but an informal pool and/or stream with stones, mosses, ferns and marginal plants and a path alongside it makes a wonderful natural garden.

Water features — The sound of water on stone has a musical simplicity that is soothing and hypnotic and a simple waterfall or fountain brings an extra dimension to the garden. The *tsukubai* or Japanese spill basin is a simple bamboo fountain and basin which was used for the ritual ablutions that formed part of the traditional tea ceremony (*tsukubai* means 'to kneel' or 'bend', referring to the humble kneeling position needed in order to wash in this basin). It involves creating a simple rocky pool (the more sheltered the better) containing a stone basin, raised above water level, and a pump. The hose is run up behind a bank of rocks and fed into a bamboo spout which emerges from the rock and is supported by two crossed bamboo poles. The water pours from the spout into the basin and from there into the pool.

Another Japanese water feature is the *shishi odoshi* or *sozu*, made of counterbalanced hollow bamboo. It was originally devised as a deer-scarer. Water is fed from a tank into a bamboo pipe which balances on a pivot over a hollow basin-like stone. When the water has filled up one end of the bamboo, it is suddenly tipped over and empties into the basin below with a musical thump. This particular water feature is easily available in kit form from garden centres.

PLANTS
Here are some suggestions for plants that might suit your Zen garden. However, as the essence of this type of garden is its stylised simplicity, it's best to choose just a few.

Trees and large shrubs — Various *Acer palmatum* (Japanese maples), *Bambus multiplex* (hedge bamboo — good for hedging and windbreaks), various Camellias, various Ceanothus, *Cornus alternifolia 'Argentea', Cornus controversa 'Variegata'* (Wedding-cake tree), Ginkgo biloba, Magnolias, *Pinus thunbergii* (Japanese black pine), various Prunus (Ornamental cherry), various Rhododendrons, *Salix 'Chrysocoma'* (Golden weeping willow), *Wisteria sinensis.*

Small shrubs and herbaceous plants — *Aciphylla squarrosa* (Bayonet plant), various Asters (Daisies, especially Michaelmas daisies), various ferns including *Phyllitis scolopendrium* (Hart's-tongue fern) and *Adiantum pedatum* (Northern maidenhair fern), various grasses including *Festuca glauca* (Blue grass), *Helictotrichon sempervirens* (Blue oat grass) and *Stipa gigantea* (Golden oats), various Hostas, *Iris sibirica*, various *Nymhaea* (Water lilies), *Phormium tenax.*

Ground cover — Various mosses, *Chamaemelum nobile* — the cultivar 'Treneague' is non-flowering and better for a lawn, *Cornus canadensis* (Creeping dogwood), *Juniperus procumbens, Lamium maculatum* 'White Nancy', *Salix reticulata* (Net-veined willow), *Soleirolia soleirolii* (Mind-your-own-business), various Thymes.

PRAYER STONES
A less elaborate but effective idea is the placing of a prayer stone or stones in the garden. In the past the cloister garden symbolised harmony and a peaceful place to pray. You can adapt this idea by choosing certain spots in your garden as places for prayer. You might make this a moving meditation, saying a particular prayer in one place and then moving on to

another place for another prayer, and so on around the garden. (If you are a Catholic you might say the Rosary in this way.) Or you might associate different parts of the garden with different aspects of your life, about which you might meditate or pray, marking each with a different stone or crystal. In this way, a rose quartz on your path might signify love and what that means to you; a clear quartz might bring you the clarity and light with which to consider a particular problem etc.

A GARDEN SHRINE

Creating a garden shrine is a lovely way of making a fixed focus for prayer and contemplation. Shrines are traditionally dedicated to specific saints or deities but can as easily be dedicated to the beauty of nature or to the sacredness intrinsic in all life — the spirit that indwells all manifestation (see the section of this book describing the native American medicine wheel for a powerful representation of this philosophy).

To make a shrine using crystals it would be a good idea to set up a four square or Star of David grid to enclose the shrine and seating area, making a sacred energy enclosure. Suitable crystals for this are roughly equal-sized clear quartz points, rough rose quartz or pieces of milky quartz (see details of these grids on pp 44). Your shrine can be as simple or as complex as you like. Start with a quiet and sheltered spot and some form of seating — even a flat-topped stone would do. For a natural shrine, a second flat stone makes a little altar on which you can place the sacred objects of your choice. You might use a cluster of clear quartz or an amethyst madonna — an arching section of amethyst geode — as the centre-piece of your altar. Stones, flowers, shells or water might have a special meaning for you and find a place on your altar.

Enclosing your shrine with sweet-smelling plants or herbs will provide extra energy. Lavender and rosemary are very cleansing, bay and myrtle carry classical associations and, for some, the scent of roses on the breeze carries with it a trace of sanctity.

A RAINBOW BRIDGE

The idea for a rainbow bridge of crystals came to me in a dream. Luckily I found it still worked on waking. More an avenue than a physical bridge, this outdoor layout uses the symbolism of a bridge — a crossing that leads you safely from one place to another — which might take you from the mundane to the meditative, from confusion to clarity or from despair to hope. You might use this layout as an approach to a shrine or a meditation garden, to one of the circles described in Chapter 15, or it might lead to a simple seat, a quiet corner or a favourite tree.

Choose your site — perhaps you have an existing path that would be suitable. Remember that you are setting up a protective avenue of transition and that the space at the other side also needs careful thought. You will need an equal number of rose quartz chunks or clear quartz points: no less than eight, but more if you want to make a long avenue. Lay the crystals in facing pairs, on each side of the path, and equally spaced about a natural stride apart, so that as you move through you will be washed with the influence of the crystals — imagine a tunnel of rainbow or rose pink light bathing you as you walk.

You could also plant creeping thymes and other sweet-smelling herbs underfoot and along the path. If you're feeling strong, you might even build a pergola to complement the crystals.

A DARK MIRROR

Water, with its wonderful depths and reflections, has always fascinated and inspired. It is a beautiful aid to meditation and was often used for scrying by psychics and shamans. You can make your own meditation pool very easily. Choose a suitable site — your pool might be set into a paved area or into the lawn or stone.

This is only a small pool, so the simplest way to start is to use a ready-made water-tight container — a large round washing-up bowl would be ideal. You should either paint the inside of this black or very dark blue with special waterproof paint or carefully line it with a black plastic bin-liner taped around the outside of the bowl (this will not show). Dig out the soil to the same size and depth as the bowl and fit the bowl in the ground to a fraction above ground level.

If you wish you can lay smooth black stones or pieces of slate on the bottom of your bowl, but this is not strictly necessary. Next, using white (milky or snowy) quartz chunks, edge your pool, making sure you have no gaps and that you have completely hidden the rim of the bowl. Fill with water. The contrast between the dark pool and the white circle is striking and makes a perfect natural seers' pool. Gaze into your pool for insight and deep reflection. You may be surprised by what you see.

CRYSTAL MAGIC

As well as creating healing contemplative spaces, crystals can help you get in touch with your fantasy. Maybe you once wondered whether fairies really danced on midsummer night or you have dreamt of seeing water nymphs and mermaids. Perhaps you always wanted to dally in a lovers' bower full of sweet scents and sounds to charm the senses. Let crystals help you bring these fantasies to life.

MIDSUMMER NIGHT'S DREAM

Imagine what fun it would be to create a summer night party out of doors with crystals illumined by candles and lanterns. If you have trees in your garden, you can create a magical effect by hanging clear quartz points from lengths of fishing line directly from the branches. You can make simple lanterns by winding fine gauge wire (copper wire is good) tightly under the rim and finishing with a long-looped wire handle. A tea light in the bottom will burn for several hours. Lanterns can also be hung from long poles pushed into the ground, but make sure they are securely fixed. Do take great care wherever you have a naked flame as there can be a risk of fire. *Never leave candles burning unattended.*

CRYSTAL LIGHTS

To make a crystal lantern, place small quartz needle point crystals with their bases embedded in Plasticine or Blu Tack inside the jar and around the tea light, hiding its metal liner and extending above it so that the candle light will shine through the crystals. Candle bases for table lighting can be made using a flower arranger's oasis on a plate. Wet the oasis, insert a tall slow-burning candle in the centre and decorate with crystal points and fragrant flower sprigs such as honeysuckle.

Hanging wind chimes and little silver bells tied to coloured ribbons will add to the magical atmosphere. If you don't have trees, try stringing a clothes line across a patio area and hanging things from that. If you get really creative you can make crystal chandeliers from clear quatz bound with copper wire and suspended from existing candlesticks, or create your own out of wire and metal. Little pieces of mirror glass behind lanterns in the flower beds will enhance the light effect. Be experimental as ordinary objects and scraps can take on a mystery and glamour at night that is lacking in daylight. Night-scented plants such as tobacco, stocks, jasmine, roses and honeysuckle will bring a heady perfume. Add good company and sweet music for a magical midsummer party.

A CRYSTAL GROTTO

A waterfall or stream running into a crystal grotto will lend enchantment to any garden. Create a grotto — a small enclosure like a natural well, perhaps partially covered on one side — using natural stones and rocks or concrete blocks covered with turf and moss. A small grotto could also be constructed from a base of well-supported moulded chicken wire, lined with black plastic sheeting into which you put earth, stones, mosses and small plants.

Ideally your grotto should be out of full sun, in cool, dappled light. Crystals suitable for a large grotto would be milky or white quartz. If you live in a granite-rich area, as I do, large amounts of white quartz are to be found about the garden and cleared to the side of fields. It would be expensive to purchase amethyst beds or clear quartz clusters sufficient for a whole grotto, but you can make a centrepiece or focus stone using something special.

The cool, green light, the scent and sound of earth and water combined with the crystal energy should entice the shyest water nymph and bring you a place of quiet refreshment for body, mind and spirit.

A LOVERS' BOWER

What could be more delightful than a quiet corner of the garden dedicated to love and its inspiration? Whether you have a small backyard or rolling acres, you can have your own lovers' bower. A seat for two is all you need, although if you are feeling ambitious you might consider a large hammock or swing instead. Rose quartz is the stone of love and its gentle, uplifting, sympathetic qualities make it the perfect basis for this creation.

Firstly decide on your location and, even if you only have a tiny space, introduce some sweet-scented plants if you can. Pots and containers can guarantee a succession of heady fragrances through the seasons, although the permanent planting of roses, jasmine and honeysuckle on an arch, enclosing a secluded bench, makes a delightful self-contained environment.

Arrange your rose quartz pieces in an enclosing grid, if you have space, or beneath the seat. Their loving and uplifting influence will be immediately felt. If you are creating a space from scratch you might consider interspersing pieces of rose quartz with cobbles to create a pattern (a star or a sun perhaps) on the floor of your bower, or perhaps scatter small rose quartz tumblestones randomly among white gravel.

CHAPTER 15

Sacred Circles

God is a circle whose centre is everywhere and
circumference nowhere

Empedocles

In so many ways the circle describes our experience of our world. Never was this more beautifully expressed than by the great sage of the Oglaga Sioux, Hehaka Sapa, otherwise known as Black Elk:

> Everything the Power of the World does is done in a circle. The sky is round, and I have heard that the earth is round like a ball, and so are all the stars. The wind, in its greatest power, whirls. Birds make their nests in circles, for theirs is the same religion as ours. The sun comes forth and goes down again in a circle. The moon does the same, and both are round.
>
> Even the seasons form a great circle in their changing, and always come back again where they were. The life of a man is a circle from childhood to childhood, and so it is in everything where power moves. Our tepees were round like the nests of birds and these were always set in a circle, the nation's hoop, a nest of many nests, where Great Spirit meant for us to hatch our children.

The grace and wisdom that such awareness can bring to our lives is always available to us, yet often we lose sight of our belonging to the 'nest of many nests' in the helter-skelter of a world that no longer dances to the pulse of the earth, honours the exquisite changes of the seasons or can see the wondrous mystery of a starry sky dimmed, as it is so often, by the glare of city lights. One way to reconnect ourselves is to make a circle of power of our own — a personal mandala — as a physical manifestation of the wholeness of life. In this chapter I look at three ways you might do this: by making a native American medicine wheel, a Celtic stone or tree circle, and a crystal spiral maze.

A MEDICINE WHEEL

In the old days when we were a strong and happy people, all our power came to us from the sacred hoop of the nation and so long as the hoop was unbroken the people flourished. The flowering tree was the living centre of the hoop, and the circle of the four quarters nourished it. The east gave peace and light, the south gave warmth, the west gave rain, and the north with its cold and mighty wind gave strength and endurance.
Hehaka Sapa, Black Elk of the Oglaga Sioux

The native American medicine wheel is a physical symbol of the created world. While it can be confusing finding your way through the differing traditions, Sioux, Cherokee, Chippewa etc. in relation to the specifics of making the wheel, nevertheless the fundamental wisdom and wholeness of the native American vision can be brought to your own creation. Medicine means power in this tradition and it is recognised that every expression of life has its own unique medicine. In creating the wheel many different powers are honoured to celebrate the hoop of creation, the Great Spirit manifesting its unity in a wonderful diversity.

Here are some of the basic principles of the medicine wheel which you can adapt according to your own feeling for the meaning and purpose of the elements of your particular circle. To create a medicine wheel in your garden, you will need a fairly flat open space, probably no less than ten feet square. Unlike the stone circle described below, you will not need very large boulders, so this is a project you can tackle yourself.

The simplest medicine wheel is made with many stones, each representing the different elements of the life of the earth — the natural world of the animals, birds, insects, fishes, plants and stones, the personal world of you, your ancestors, your family and friends, and the collective worlds of religions, governments, institutions and philosophies. The great powers of earth, sun, moon and stars might also have a place on your wheel.

Begin by marking out a circle, using two poles and a length of twine. If you are making a wheel with a diameter of 10 feet, then the twine needs to be attached to each pole allowing a full 5 feet length to hang between. Fix one pole in the earth at the place you have chosen to be the centre of your wheel and then describe your circle by moving out to the length of the twine and scraping the ground with the second stick as you walk a full circle. Try to keep the stick upright, otherwise you may end up with an oval.

Next, with the help of a compass, mark the four points, north, south, east and west, on the circumference and mark out a line bisecting the circle north to south and then a second line crossing it east to west. You should end up with a cross within the circle. This is the ground plan of your basic wheel.

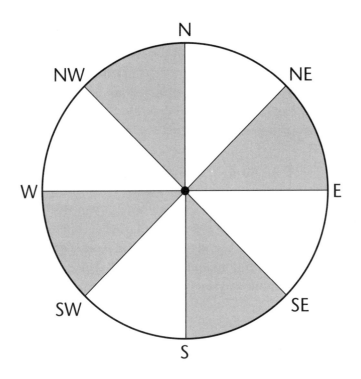

Medicine wheel layout

Before covering your layout with stones it's a good idea
to think about their meaning to you and the significance of
their placement. You might, for example, decide these hand-
fuls of stones represent the four legged peoples, those pebbles
the creepie-crawlies, the finned or the winged, and so forth,
as a first step in covering the wheel, before deciding where
to put individual stones and crystals that represent the individuals and elements of key significance to you at this time.

THE BEAUTY WAY

Each of the directions has its traditional attributes:

The north — gateway to the mind. It is designated the place of the stars, the mind, age and wisdom. Its totem or power animal is the buffalo, its element is air, its colour is white, its season is winter, its time period is the future and it is the place of philosophy, science and religion. The enemy of the mind is certainty.

The south — gateway to the emotions and it is the place of the moon, youth, trust and innocence. Its totem is the mouse, its element water, its colour red, its season summer. Its time is the past and it is the place of music. The enemy of the emotions is fear.

The east — gateway to the spirit. It is the place of the sun, illumination and enlightenment. Its totem is the eagle, its element fire, its colour yellow, its season spring. Its time is the moment and it is the place of art and writing. The enemy of the spirit is death.

The west — gateway to the body. It is the place of the earth, intuition and introspection, change and transition. Its totem is the bear, its element earth, its colour black, its season autumn. Its time is the present and it is the place of magic. The enemy of the body is powerlessness.

The centre — the eye of the creator and the heart of the cosmos, the centre of love and light. Its totem is the breath/smoke, its element ether, its colours blue-green and magenta-violet. Its time period is timelessness and it is the place of spirituality.

Between the fixed points on the wheel are the pathways which represent the many journeys of life, both inner and outer, as well as the movements of night to day to night, the changing seasons and the turning of the earth and the planets around the sun. Moving on the pathways around the wheel can bring deeper meaning to your experience of these cycles in your life.

Along the pathways there are also positions associated with different functions and qualities. When you move inwards along the pathway from the north to the centre, you move through the places of cleansing, renewal and purity on your journey to the centre. Moving inwards along the pathway from east to centre, you find clarity, wisdom and illumination. Walking the pathway from south to centre, you connect with growth, trust and love; and from west to centre you meet experience, introspection and strength.

When you create your wheel you might like to choose a crystal to represent yourself, different stones for the members of your family and ancestors. Traditionally, important stones or crystals are chosen to represent Father Sun, Mother Earth and Grandmother Moon. These are placed in the wheel near the centre, the place of the creator — this perhaps signified by a beautiful quartz sphere, point or cluster or, if your wheel is permanent, by the planting of a flowering tree. When you have chosen a crystal to represent yourself, it is interesting to move it around and experience the movement of that crystal on the wheel. How does it feel to be standing in this place? What are its lessons? What is its medicine? In this way the wheel can become a powerful tool for self-development and discovery.

From this very brief summary you can see that the medicine wheel has the potential for becoming a very powerful place for you, a place of moving meditation and possible transformation. You will find suggestions for further reading at the back of the book. Native Americans refer to living with consciousness and respect for life as the 'Beauty Way'. The creation of a medicine wheel can help you walk in beauty.

HEALING HERBS

A beautiful development of the medicine wheel is to plant different healing herbs within the wheel or at the points of power on the wheel. Similar use could be made of a sacred wheel for the cultivation of fruits and vegetables. The use of any sacred space for growing plants will greatly enhance the energy and efficacy of the plant. Let your imagination and the crystals guide you.

AN IRISH STONE CIRCLE

I invoke thee Erin,
Brilliant, brilliant river,
Fertile, fertile hill,
Wavy, wavy wood,
Flowing, flowing stream,
Fishy, fishy lake.

Amergin, the Milesian poet, from the *Book of Leinster*.

Of the many prehistoric stone circles found in Ireland, the small circles of the south-west are among the most delightful. Many of these circles follow a similar layout and alignment and it is this basic design that we followed for the stone circle in our own garden, originally created for a celebration of blessing following the marriage of one of my stepdaughters. It has a timeless and grounding energy and, although the circle is only two years old, it looks and feels as if it has always been there.

To build a stone circle in your garden, you will need a suitable open space from 10 to 30 feet square and nine or thirteen large stones. Granite boulders are ideal as they often have a high proportion of quartz in them, which will make them very energetic. It might be advisable to call on some professional help for this project. Among the useful addresses at the back of this book I have listed the company which helped us to erect our circle.

Plan your layout carefully in advance with the help of a compass, a pole and a length of twine. Fix the pole, with the twine attached, in the centre of your site — the radius of your circle will determine the length of twine you use. You can then describe your circle with a line of silver sand or powdered chalk. Use a compass to mark out the positions of the stones.

The recumbent stone, a low flatish stone, is placed in the south-west. Directly opposite, in the north-east, is the entrance of the circle, marked by the two tallest uprights, known as portal stones. The remaining stones are placed, usually in descending order of height in each direction from the entrance to the recumbent, at an equal distance apart. With nine stones you have a stone to mark each of the eight directions (the two portal stones standing in place of one).

Using thirteen stones you mark out the cross-quarter directions and the twelve months/moons of the year, again with two stones at either side of the entrance marking the place of one. In each year there are twelve full lunar cycles, but there are in fact thirteen full or new moons, so if you are working with these you still have the stones you need. Using thirteen stones the cardinal points (north, south, east and west) are actually marked by the space between the stones which may then also serve as portals or symbolic openings to the energies associated with the particular direction. (See diagrams page 161.)

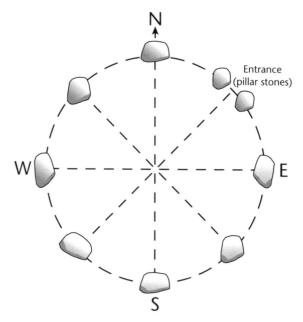

Nine stone circle

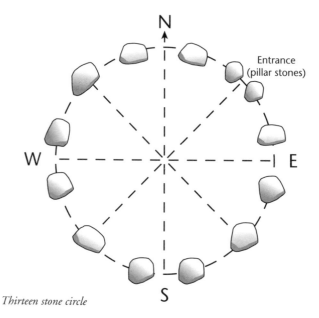

Thirteen stone circle

MAGICAL NUMBERS

Nine and thirteen are both magical numbers. Nine is the flipside of one. It is about the power of giving away power, the pleasure of giving. St Francis reminds us: 'It is in giving that we receive.' The service of humanity is paramount in working with nine, either by directly serving others or through creative expression. Nine is associated with the mysteries of relationship between the *self* and the *all*, microcosm and macrocosm.

Thirteen is often thought to be unlucky. While this superstition is often attributed to the number present at the Last Supper, it is undoubtedly also a hangover from the time when the Christian Church wished to purge many of the pagan customs of the Celtic peoples. As I've already mentioned, there are always either thirteen full or new moons in one calendar year and the moon and her cycles was a key part of Celtic life, symbolising the tides of life, when to sow and when to reap.

The moon was representative of the triple goddess, the new moon seen as the Maiden, a willowy girl, the full moon, the pregnant Mother aspect of the goddess, and the old moon represented the Crone or wise one. The time of the waxing or increasing moon (from new to full) was the time for creating, planting, beginnings and new enterprises. The waning moon (from full until the next new moon) was the time for retreating, moving inwards, completion and contemplation. With the powerful resurgence of Celtic spirituality we are reconnecting once more with these natural tides and cycles.

THE CELTIC CALENDAR

While the places of the solstices and equinoxes belong in the four quarters on the Celtic calendar (north — winter solstice, south — summer solstice, east — spring equinox and west — autumn equinox), the four great festivals of the Celtic year fall in between at the cross-quarters. At north-east is the festival of Imbolc on 1 February, at south-east is Beltane on 1 May, at south-west is Lugnasadh on 1 August and at north-west is Samain on 1 November.

The Festival of Imbolc (1 February) — meaning 'ewe's milk'. Associated with the goddess *Brighid*, St Brigid (2 February), the time of births and childhood. The sensing of new life emerging and the approach of spring.

The Festival of Beltane (1 May) — a great Celtic festival marking the beginning of summer and *an ghrian mor*, the great sun, which is the period between *Beltane* and *Samain*. The old customs of choosing a May queen and maypole dancing are remnants of this celebration. A time to celebrate youthful vigour, beauty and passion. The entrance to the Otherworld of the fairy folk and the *sidhe* is believed to be wide open at this time.

The Festival of Lugnasadh (1 August) — the harvest time, named for the god *Lugh*, but also known as Lammas, from the Anglo-saxon *hlaef-mas*, the Mass Loaf. In Ireland this has always been the great time for trading, horse fairs, community games and tribal get-togethers. In Celtic custom it was the time for assessing the worthiness of leaders, chiefs and kings by the success of the harvest. Therefore *Lugnasadh* is the time of reaping what has been sown, adult responsibilities and evaluations.

The Festival of Samain (1 November) — the beginning of the Celtic new year, the sowing of seeds, the honouring of the ancestors — which is incorporated into the Christian festival of All Souls — and a moving into communion with the inner worlds. *Samain* marked the start of *an ghrian beag*, the little sun, which ruled until the next *Beltane*. Once again the entrance to the Otherworld is believed to be open and the ancestors and the *sidhe* walk abroad. The tradition of dressing up and masking at Hallowe'en came from the belief that it was safer to confuse the spirits, lest you were taken. A time of clearing out and letting go, of storytelling and honouring the elders.

The associations of the cardinal quarters with certain qualities and energies is somewhat different in the Celtic tradition than those associated with the medicine wheel.

East is the quarter of air and is associated with dawn, springtime and renewal.
South is the place of fire and is associated with noon, summer, light, heat, change and growth.
West is the place of water and is associated with twilight, autumn, fertility, maturity and the moon and tides.
North is the place of earth, associated with night, winter, cold, wisdom and strength.

John Matthews, in his excellent book, *The Celtic Shaman*, marks the pathways between these eight directions in this way: between the portals at north-east (*Imbolc*) and the east (spring equinox) are snowdrops; between east and south-east (*Beltane*) are bluebells; between south-east and south (summer solstice) is hawthorn; between south and south-west (*Lugnasadh*) is wheat; between south-west and west (autumn equinox) are apples; between west and north-west

(*Samain*) are autumn leaves; between north-west and north (winter solstice) is bare earth; and between north and north-east is snow.

The hawthorn, May tree or fairy thorn is revered as sacred in Ireland and is often found in or near a stone circle. If you build your own stone circle you might consider planting a hawthorn tree in the south-south-east of your circle; similarly an apple tree at west-south-west; another tree (perhaps a rowan) at west-north-west, with snowdrops and bluebells in their places.

In the centre you might like to place a special crystal — my choice would be a lovely natural quartz point of a large piece of rose quartz — to mark the place of spirit, the still centre on which your day, your year, your life turns and returns.

You can use your stone circle in similar ways to the medicine wheel, as you stand at different points around or within the circle. Standing at the centre you will feel the energy and pull of the different elements and influences of the turning world around you.

A TREE CIRCLE

An alternative to making a stone circle is to make a circle entirely of trees, marking each of the festivals and quarters with a special tree associated with that time. Trees are very sacred in the Celtic tradition and there is great meaning attached to the growth and habit of different native trees. When planting each tree you might plant an appropriately dedicated crystal at its roots. Here are some suggestions:

> East: alder or ash (garnet or citrine)
> South-east: hawthorn (rose quartz)
> South: oak (diamond or agate)

South-west: hazel or apple (topaz)

West: willow or ivy (aquamarine, opal or fluorite)

North-west: elder or elm (amethyst or sapphire)

North: holly or yew (obsidian or quartz)

North-east: rowan or birch, two trees if you wish to make a portal (carnelian or tourmaline)

Be aware that the needs and habits of these trees vary when you are choosing a site — willow, for example, needs plenty of moisture. It is worth doing a bit of research and planning before you start digging. However, with a little patience, you will have created your own sacred grove, a sanctuary and a living testament to the world around you.

THE SPIRAL MAZE: A SACRED SPIRAL WALK

*Walking into the centre of the spiral I return to
the source of creation.
Walking out, I remake my world with golden thread
spun from my heart .*
Traditional ritual

The spiral is a very effective form for a moving meditation and, unlike the circles described previously, it is the actual experience of walking it (most effectively blindfold or with eyes closed, if you have someone to guide you) that changes your reality, without reference to symbols or markers. It is a great deal less grounded than the cross-quartered circles and is more of an experiential machine for altering consciousness. Care should be taken if you are already inclined to be 'away with the fairies'.

Using nine key stones you can make a powerful spiral walking maze. The spiral form expresses much of the energy of nine (see the notes in the section on the Celtic circle for the significance of the number nine). The energy spirals inwards to the centre and then returns back to the whole of creation in a constant dance or double helix. Spiralling energy is more feminine and intuitive than masculine and constructive. The nine sisters at the cauldron of Cerridwen, the nine Muses and in Arthurian legend the nine sisters on the Isle of Avalon give us a sense of the archetypal significance and feminine power spun by the spiral of nine.

If you want to create a spiral maze, start by marking out the spiral on the ground (follow the illustration) with the help of a compass and a ball of twine. Without this guide you can get in a muddle. The diameter for the complete spiral should be as large as space allows but, ideally, at least 12 feet.

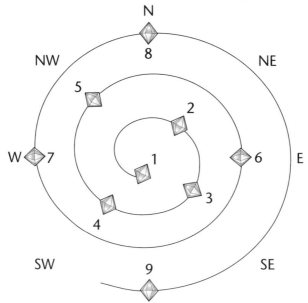

Spiral Maze (using nine crystals)

Next, using nine large crystals, start with crystal 1 at the centre. Moving outwards and clockwise, place 2 in the north-east. Continue clockwise to place 3 in the south-east, 4 in the south-west and continuing outwards, 5 in the north-west. Move out and round to place 6 in the east, 7 in the west, 8 in the north and lastly 9 at the outer edge in the south.

For a very strong focus to the centre, using quartz points, place the crystals facing anticlockwise along the path of the spiral towards the centre. For a dispersing energy place the crystal points facing clockwise. Turning them all to the centre will concentrate the energy on the inner; facing the crystals outwards will broadcast energy and give more emphasis to the return. Experiment and see which suits you best. It will very much depend on the purpose you intend. A gentler and very lovely grid could be made using pieces of rough rose quartz. Yet another variation could be to use clusters or a cluster at the centre, or a combination of any of these.

Working with the spiral will open you up to the mysteries, the nature of life and reality. The spiral form is very powerful and it will quite radically alter your perceptions of time and space. As you move slowly along the pathway to the centre, you seem to travel a vast distance and lose all sense of time. At the centre you will *become* the meeting point between the upper and lower worlds and the eye which sees through to other realms of reality. When you are ready, make your way out of the spiral clockwise, bringing the wisdom or awareness you have contacted out with you into the world. There is a meditation in Chapter 19 which you can use with the spiral maze.

This layout can be made permanent in various ways. If you have an area of lawn which you are prepared to give over to the spiral maze, you could mow the spiral form (mowing into the centre in an anticlockwise direction and out again along the same path), establishing it over 3–4 cuts, keeping the pathway close cut and the in-between high cut. You can inset your stones in the lawn (deeply enough not to interfere with mowing), but it's perhaps better to lay them out whenever you wish to use the crystal spiral as they can get lost or overgrown.

Alternatively, mark out the whole spiral form in a continuous line of plain cobbles, with the nine key stones standing out distinctively. Rose quartz looks beautiful among pale grey or white cobbles. You might consider making this design part of a fully paved area of the garden.

SECTION V

Crystals and Inner Space

It is only with the heart that one can see rightly;
What is essential is invisible to the eye.
Antoine de Saint-Exupery

CHAPTER 16

Crystal Dreaming

I have spread my dreams under your feet;
Tread softly because you tread on my dreams.

W. B. Yeats

Many shamanic cultures value dreaming highly as a way of bringing balance and wisdom to ordinary life. In our own society, Sigmund Freud described our dreams as 'the royal road to a knowledge of the unconscious activities of the mind' and Carl Jung took Freud's pioneering work and dedicated much of his brilliant life to developing dream analysis as a route to understanding the psyche. If you are interested in learning more from your dreams, crystals can help you to access and remember them by enhancing your awareness and intuitition and by opening doorways into this extended reality.

WORKING WITH YOUR DREAMS

The custom of recounting and working with dreams underpins the culture of the Senoi, a tribe living in the mountains of Malaysia. The Senoi are remarkable for one unique achievement — crime is virtually unknown within their community and they are rarely troubled by their neighbours, due to a reputation for being powerful magicians. At the beginning of each day throughout their lives, starting in early childhood, every family member recounts his/her dreams. Their methods are simple, but clearly most effective. If you would like to try the Senoi approach for yourself, the basic rules for dream behaviour are essentially as follows:

1. Confront and conquer danger. Instead of running away from what feels dangerous in a dream, the child (or adult) is encouraged to confront and conquer danger — fighting if necessary and calling on dream helpers for assistance as required. When conquered you demand a gift (perhaps a song or a poem) to bring back into waking life. Recognise that the power of your enemies is your power which they have stolen, so the more powerful your enemy, the more powerful you are. If attacked by friends, remember they are spirits wearing the mask of your friend's appearance. However, make an effort in waking life to renew your friendship so the spirit cannot damage your relationship.
2. Advance towards pleasure. If this is sexual, move through to orgasm. Don't worry about incestuous or other forbidden liaisons as the dream lover is simply wearing a reassuring and familiar mask. Request a gift afterwards to represent the love and pleasure between you.
3. Achieve a positive result. If you are falling, try flying. Find out where the spirits want you to go. Explore the new environment and take careful note of it. Keep a careful lookout for anything that might be of value in your waking life.

REMEMBERING YOUR DREAMS
Each new day is the beginning of a new adventure in life which will always be different — challenging, tranquil, sublime, unexpected, exciting or low key. You will enhance the spirit of your daytime adventure if you start each day by capturing your dreams, the memories of your night-time adventure. By forgetting your dreams you forget possibly the most creative third of your life.

To help you to remember your dreams more easily you might try all or any of the following tips:

- Keep a notebook or journal for your dreams, with pen and light beside your bed.
- Clear your head by reviewing the events of the day before going to sleep. It will clear your head for a dream the next morning.
- As you fall asleep tell yourself that you intend to write down your dreams first thing next morning.
- Write the first thing that comes to you on waking, dream or not, uncensored, and write down all your dreams — even the worst. We are total beings, not good or bad. Your dreams reveal all — it's the things you want to avoid that you most often need to look at.
- Write down dream fragments, not just the most vivid or exciting dreams, and always in as much detail as possible.
- Note any feelings you have in your dreams and their feel tone (e.g. dangerous situation but felt very comfortable).
- Use a key word to trigger dream recall. Give yourself a trigger word which you decide on before you go to sleep, telling yourself that when you repeat it on waking you will remember your dreams.
- Don't wake with an alarm or music as it will instantly change your consciousness. Train yourself to wake just before the alarm, in anticipation of your new day.
- Don't move, get out of bed or exercise on waking.
- Relax and let yourself fail. Stress and anxiety to achieve will sabotage results.

- Be in tune with your bed partner. It is easier if you both keep dream notebooks, although it's important that neither reads the other's journal — not only is this inhibiting but also an invasion of privacy.
- An event or news item from the day before may trigger a dream, but remember it is you who makes the selection from thousands of different impressions, so it will have some significance for you.
- Tell yourself that your dreams are important. They are a significant part of your total life experience.

DREAM CRYSTALS

A piece of rose quartz or a Herkimer diamond can assist your dream recall. On going to bed, connect with your crystal, asking it to store your dreams for you. Place it under the pillow. On waking (try not to shift from your sleeping position or even open your eyes), reach for the crystal and tune in.

PROTECTING YOUR DREAM SPACE

You can set up a protective energy grid around your bed with the specific purpose of bringing protection while you dream — a four square grid or Star of David created with rose quartz would be particularly gentle and comforting. For a more focused energy, activate a crystal for the specific function of becoming your dream guardian. Cleanse and energise the crystal in the usual way (see Chapter 4), then formulate the exact purpose you have in mind for your crystal. It might be to protect you during sleep, for example, or maybe to help you have lucid dreams or dreams of particular power. In a state of peace and receptivity ask your crystal to assist you in this task. You will learn from experience that some crystals offer themselves readily for a particular purpose, while others may seem quite reluctant and unresponsive. This may sound fanciful, but do try to be sensitive to your crystals and allow them to speak to you.

Other physical protections might take the form of a crystal-decorated shamanic shield or a dream net or dreamcatcher hung above the bed. A crystal-energised dreamcatcher will also bring protection from nightmares and a good energy to your bedroom. (For instructions on how to make your own, see the project on page 93.)

VIVID DREAMS

The following visualisation exercise removes mental clutter and has the double benefit of making your dreams more vivid and promoting positive change in your life, especially where old habits have caused stagnation. It needs to be done with a partner. Take turns to be both listener and cleaner. The listener reads the exercise — very slowly and allowing time for a descriptive response — prompting when necessary and requesting as many details as possible in order to make the experience really vivid to the cleaner. Hold a clear quartz crystal point away from you in your clearing hand (see Chapter 6) while you are cleaning.

Exercise: Cleaning your Head

Make yourself comfortable and close your eyes.

Select the room in your own home that you are going to clean.

Decide what equipment you will use.

You can have anything — buckets, sprays, detergents, soap, step ladders etc.

Describe your room to me *in as much detail as possible* and your choice of equipment.

Start with ceiling and clean it, then go down the walls.
As you reach pictures, book cases etc., describe them.
Now clean them and move them so you can clean behind
them.
If necessary move furniture into the centre of the room.
As you clean, decide what items you are going to keep
and what you are going to throw out.
Put what you no longer want outside the door.
Small items can go in a packing case.
Larger items can just be piled up in a heap.
Clean carpet and floor.
When you have finished, clean and put back each item
you wish to keep, describing each one.
Double check what you want to throw out.
Now imagine that you go outside and burn the rubbish in
a cleansing bonfire,
or tip it in a lake of healing water which transforms every-
thing it receives.

LUCID DREAMING

You may be interested in developing your ability to have lucid
dreams. A lucid dream is a dream in which you realise you
are dreaming but can't wake up. It is something that can give
you access to a world of astonishing plasticity and responsive-
ness. If you notice the dream is in black and white, demand
colour and the dreamscape instantly turns into technicolor.
You want to fly, you find you are instantly soaring above the
ground.

Choose a quartz crystal and effect a close link with it by
doing the meditation *Entering the Crystal* on page 186. Hold
and connect with your crystal as you fall asleep and, because
you know that crystals have the same structure and

appearance in the dreamworld as they do in waking reality, you form a conscious intention of looking for your crystal again in your dream state. When you recover your crystal in your dream, it will remind you that you are dreaming and at this point you should go lucid, that is, you will become conscious while still dreaming. Holding a lucid state requires lots of practice — when I was first aware of lucid dreaming, I became so excited that I woke myself up.

CHAPTER 17

Crystals and Meditation

To see a world in a grain of sand,
And heaven in a wild flower,
Hold infinity in the palm of your hand,
And eternity in an hour.

William Blake

Meditation and crystals are both tools to assist us on the journey of life. Both help us to live more consciously in each moment. Meditation is an age-old technique for quietening the everyday mind, for turning the attention to touch a sacred inner place of peace, wisdom and guidance.

WHY USE CRYSTALS?

Crystals will transform and balance energy fields, bringing a helpful harmony to the environment in which you meditate by creating a sacred space, as well as helping you to enhance inner awareness by developing your right brain intuitive faculty. Crystals also store information which will help you to return to a previously achieved meditative state much more easily. If you wish to use a crystal in this way, you should keep one specifically for meditation and personal development. Choose one that appeals to you (I would recommend the quartz group) and cleanse and bless it in the way outlined in Chapter 4.

CREATING A MEDITATION SPACE

As in all things, the outer environment is both a reflection of and also an influence on the inner state. So it is important to have a peaceful, undisturbed environment for meditation — at least until you are so proficient that your whole life becomes a meditation! If at all possible, keep a little room or even the *corner* of a room specifically for meditation. Find a space where you can be alone without interruption.

Begin by thoroughly cleaning the space you have chosen. Next, you can use one of the crystal grids outlined in Chapter 5 to create a sacred space of the appropriate energy. If you have a whole room, I would suggest a simple four square grid, that is, a little crystal point in each corner. A Star of David grid around your chair will bring you a beautifully supportive energy of balance and alignment. Whether you prefer a simple environment or to decorate it with a few well-chosen objects that contribute to your sense of sacred space, is up to you. Flowers, candles, artwork, music or incense might inspire serenity in some but be distracting to others.

Before starting your meditation always turn off the phone and anything else that could interrupt you.

LEARNING TO RELAX

The health benefits of a relaxed body and mind are legion and you have to learn to relax if you want to meditate. Choose an upright position that will not automatically induce sleep unless your meditation is in preparation for dreaming. Having a straight spine means that your *chakras* (see Chapter 6) are aligned, earth to crown, and your energy can flow unobstructed. When we are feeling vulnerable and un-relaxed, we often close off the energy flow by crossing our legs and arms in an instinctive gesture of self-protection.

It is a matter of practical preference whether you sit cross-legged on the floor (or, for the yoga practitioner, in a half or full lotus) or in an upright chair. But it is important to choose a sitting position which you can comfortably maintain for between half and three-quarters of an hour. Your spine should be straight and well supported. The chair, which is the best choice for most people, should be straight backed, without arms and of average height, allowing you to have both feet hip-width apart and flat on the floor, with knees bent at 90°. Legs are best uncrossed as energy can then move freely and you have a good contact with the ground. (Sitting on the ground with straight spine will give a similar grounding as the base *chakra* is in contact with the ground.) Shoulders should be dropped and relaxed, arms comfortably by your sides, and your hands resting softly in your lap.

When you are ready to begin, check your body for muscle tension, especially your neck, shoulders and buttocks. To relax tight muscles, tense the affected areas even more tightly, hold until it's uncomfortable, then release completely. If you wish you can record the following relaxation exercise (or an adaptation of your own) to play through as preparation for your meditation.

Exercise: Love and Bless your Body

How often do you send loving thoughts to your body?
You are going to start to send love to your body
so that your body can relax and let go
of tensions, tiredness, aches and pains.
Make sure you are sitting comfortably and close your eyes.
Bring your attention to your feet.
Let warm blessing and love caress your feet.
Stroke to blessing over the instep and heel
around your ankles and into your calves.

Feel the love and appreciation flowing up your legs to your knees.

Bless your knees.

Now feel the warmth and relaxation softening the long muscles of your thighs.

Your buttocks and tummy muscles relax as they are filled with the warmth of your blessing. Love your tummy.

Let the relaxation flow up your spine and across your shoulders.

Shrug off any burdens you have carried there.

Feel your shoulders relax and drop.

Now feel the love and blessing flowing down your arms to your hands.

Your hands are miraculous tools for giving, receiving, creating, comforting.

Love and bless your hands.

Bring your attention to your neck.

Feel that your neck is being stroked with love.

Keep your neck relaxed and free, long at the back, tucking your chin down slightly

so you can feel your neck long and free.

And stroke the love up to your head.

Feel the little muscles relaxing across your scalp. Bless your brain.

Love your face. You have a unique and beautiful face.

Bless your senses, bless your lovely eyes and the gift of sight.

Bless your ears and the wonderful range of sounds they bring

the sound of the wind in the trees, the laughter of children, music.

Bless your nose and the richness of scents you experience.

Bless your mouth and tongue for speech and for all the
taste and savour of life.

Love and bless your whole body.

Imagine it surrounded and bathed in a bubble of light,
light which is love.

Your body is perfectly protected, healthy and whole.

BREATH IS LIFE

The next vital preparation for meditation is your breathing.
Establish an easy rhythm, slow but comfortable, and allow
yourself to observe your own breathing for a few minutes as
your busy mind quietens. A useful technique is to count your
breathing for a few minutes as follows:

Inhale for a count of four.

Hold the breath for a count of two.

Exhale for a count of four

and pause for a count of two

before inhaling again for a count of four.

You can vary the length of the breaths according to your
ability and comfort to, say, six and three or eight and four. Do
not strain. This is not a competition.

If you find distracting thoughts flitting into your mind,
just allow them to float past, as if on an inner screen, and then
off again. This peaceful non-anxiety will settle you better
than any amount of effort. Trying to meditate, to let go or to
push away thoughts is always counter-productive and holds
you in a state of anxiety.

Another wonderful exercise is to breathe light into the
heart centre. This has the effect of expanding inner awareness and connectedness to the sacred. Hold your personal
crystal to your heart to enhance the sense of light.

An Irish Stone Circle (Chapter 15): *The author at the centre of the thirteen-stone circle in her garden, with mown, spiral walk and rose quartz placements (the flat recumbent stone top left of the circle marks south-east, the thirteenth stone is hidden behind the taller portal stone at right of the picture).*

Making a healing frame or mirror (Chapter 9)

Rainbow bright tumblestones (*Chapter 9*): *Little piles* (from left to right) *of unakite, hematite, Botswana agate, snowflake obsidian, tiger eye and rose quartz. In the spiral* (from centre, outwards) *jasper, carnelian, citrine, aventurine* (clearer) *and amazonite* (opaque, brighter green), *blue lace agate, sodalite, amethyst, white and clear quartz.*

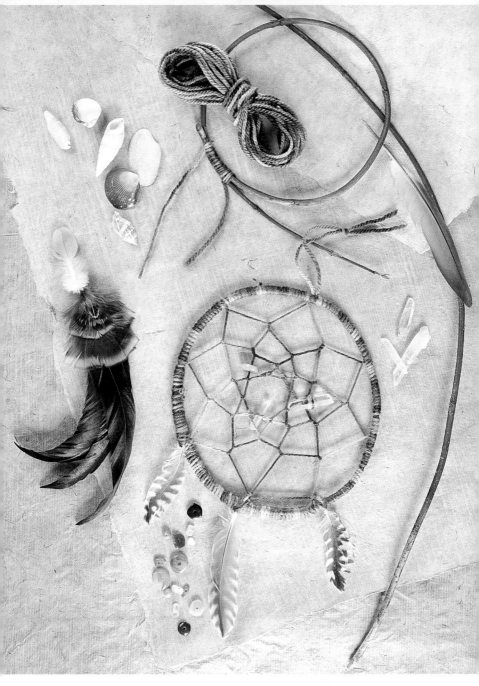

Only let the good dreams through (Chapter 9): *A dreamcatcher above your bed will catch the bad dreams.*

Energy and light (Chapter 2): *Natural clear quartz points from around the world. Some different natural formations (from top left): Brazilian 'tabular' quartz point laid over Madagascar point and Arkansas 'laser wand', Madagascar 'needle' point, three Brazilian double terminated points, Brazilian crystal 'twins', large Madagascar single point, small Brazilian cluster, double terminated Madagascar quartz.*

Amethyst at the threshold (Chapter 7)

Bottling and labelling gem elixirs (*Chapter 6*): *Preserve your stock bottles of gem waters in brandy, label clearly and store in a cool, dark place.*

Crystal energised water (*Chapter 6*): *Orange calcite in a glass bowl of spring water placed outside for twenty-four hours (ideally around full moon) to get the balance of sun and moon influences.*

Green, blue and turquoise stones (from top right, spiralling clockwise): *Tiny emerald tumbles, malachite tumbles, obelisk and triangular polished piece, two watermelon tourmaline slices and small natural piece, aventurine tumbles, jade tumbles and slices, kyanite pieces, two aquamarine tumbles, two amazonite tumbles, small peridot tumbles, chrysocolla druse and polished, apophyllite cluster, turquoise pieces, blue lace agate tumbles, fluorite—polished sphere, two palm stones and an octahedron.*

White, pink and rutilated stones (from top left): *Rough rose quartz, rose quartz tumbles, rose quartz crystal, moonstone tumbles, rubellite (pink tourmaline) in its matrix rock, opal, morganite* (pink beryl), *calcite cluster with stilbite* (peach coloured), *two large herkimer diamonds, selenite sheet, selenite with inclusions and encrustations, rutilated quartz tumbles and prism, two girasol quartz pebbles, small clear quartz cluster.*

Exercise: Light Heartedness
Focus on your breathing and allow your breath
to become a little slower and deeper than usual,
nice and easy and regular with no strain,
just a sense of flowing with the rhythm of air and lungs.
Enjoy this physical experience for a few moments.

Now imagine that every in-breath expands your heart
centre outwards,
rather like bellows,
so that progressively the heart centre is expanding
according to your breathing.
At the same time, see the breath as very sparkling,
clear light-energy, so that the heart is becoming filled
with more and more light.

Do this light-heart breathing for a few minutes until you
sense an inner peace and light as a slight buzz of energy
in your chest. If you can do this exercise outside in a
natural and peaceful setting, so much the better, then you
will find it even quicker and easier to attain light-
heartedness.

I have outlined below some different forms of meditation
which you might like to try. Different approaches suit different people. Experiment to find which way is best for you.
Please remember these are only guidelines which you can
adapt to suit yourself. You will find that all meditation begins
with relaxation and good breathing.

1. ACTIVE ATTENTION

The simplest (and most difficult) form of meditation is to become completely open to presence and stillness — an active attentiveness to being, not doing but not a passive condition either. It awakens and exercises 'inner muscles', which will respond to steady and patient practice. A very pure form of this technique is expressed in Zen Buddhism, that is, Zen mind as the beginner's mind in which there are many possibilities, whereas in the expert's mind there are but few. In the words of the Christian mystic, Meister Eckhart, 'The eye with which I see God is the same eye with which God sees me.' And at the heart of the Tibetan *Book of the Dead* we discover the living realisation that 'This is That.'

You can use your crystal to help you on this journey towards ultimate simplicity. Ultimately you may discover that you and the crystal are one. The following exercise is one I use often and it is based on a meditation given by Pamela Chase and Jonathan Pawlik in *The Newcastle Guide to Healing with Crystals*. If you are serious about using a crystal for personal development and increased awareness, this meditation links you with the crystal's essence most effectively. Unless you have a friend to read for you, it's a good idea to record the meditations on to a cassette which you can play back. The key is to relax and take it slowly, allowing good long pauses between each line of the meditation.

Exercise: Entering the Crystal

Sit upright and make sure you are warm, comfortable and relaxed. Remember, it is best to have your legs uncrossed and placed flat on the ground or floor. Hold your crystal in your receiving hand, or in both hands, and allow yourself to become quiet and receptive, breathing regularly and slowly.

With thoughts of pure love and light ask your crystal to open an area of its structure so you may enter its perfect form.

See your crystal make a special space for you.

Enter your crystal through the doorway of light provided for you.

Feeling in a state of perfect balance, you choose to explore the interior of your crystal.

Allow all your senses to be open to experience your crystal.

Touch its sides, its foundation, with your face, your hands.

Allow your body to lean against a crystal wall.

Listen to any sounds you may hear.

Feel you are at home and totally welcomed by your crystal.

Spend a little while enjoying the attunement.

Now prepare to leave.

Thank your crystal for sharing its energies with you.

Re-focus on your breathing, wiggle your hands and feet and return to the present.

Open your eyes.

Entering the Crystal can be used in a lot of different ways. It is a fundamental tool in preparation for any deep crystal work and all the meditation exercises that follow. It also provides a good basis for further meditations you can devise yourself.

2. CONTEMPLATION

Contemplation is a classical form of meditation and a favoured technique of many Western and Eastern religious orders. This method usually involves intelligent, open attentiveness to a seed thought, a text or an object. At its best it will centre you and bring insight and greater clarity to the mind. By using a crystal to help you achieve a quiet mind, you can become more aware of what is most ordinary and familiar to you, helping you to re-experience yourself as connected to all life.

Remembering is an exercise based on contemplation which involves becoming aware of what is happening *right now*, whatever the circumstances, wherever you are. Do this for just a few moments and you will be amazed by what you discover. If you hold a personal crystal (usually a clear quartz point or piece of rose quartz) in your receiving hand (see page 52), it will make tuning in to this exercise easier, as the crystal will enhance your awareness.

Exercise: Remembering (Re-membering)

You will become aware of sounds
you had not previously noticed
— those that are close by
and those that are further away.
You will notice how your body feels.
Is it warm or cool . . . heavy or light . . . relaxed or aching?
Perhaps it is different in different parts.
You will become aware of your breathing
and certain scents.

It can be helpful to close your eyes
for your eyes tend to be your most developed,
your most relied-upon sense.
So it is easy to become lazy about what you see.
To go unconscious and be on automatic
by initially closing out the sense of sight,
you become more sensitive to the stimuli of your other senses.

After you have gathered as much information as possible with your eyes closed,
open them and you will be surprised to note
that certain things now appear somewhat changed to you.

If you do this several times each day, you will find it beneficially affects your perceptions and memory. You will literally be remembering yourself in relationship to the *all* and *everything* and this gradually becomes a natural condition.

Exercise: The Perfect Being in the Heart

This is a famous exercise for centring yourself. I am grateful to William Bloom whose book, *Meditation in a Changing World,* provided me with this and many other valuable exercises and insights which we continue to use regularly in our meditation group in Tullow. With regular practice, you will notice that the contemplation of an inner image of perfection brings noticeable and beneficial changes to your life.

Become relaxed and calm.
Allow your posture and breathing to bring you to a place of peace.
Now imagine the person who carries your ideal qualities of mystical and divine perfection.
This may be a famous religious figure, Christ or Buddha, for example.
Or it may be a figure who is totally private to you.
Don't worry if you don't visualise easily.
You need only have a sense of this person
and the energy that is generated.

Sense the appearance of the figure,
the beautiful and the perfect atmosphere which radiates
from it.
Now imagine the figure being placed within your own
heart.
The figure sits in your heart.
You sense its effects as you contemplate this image of
perfection that has now become aligned with you.
In perfect serenity and poise, contemplate the beauty of
this union.

You can also use this technique to contemplate a difficult
issue in your life, by placing the issue in front of you, bathed
in white light, and merely observing what is there. Insight
and a shifted viewpoint can often emerge. Give it time and
withhold judgment — loving detachment seems to be the
key attitude.

3. INNER WISDOM
Meditation can take the form of becoming still and opening
yourself up to inner help and guidance. The following
exercise is based on the meditation, *Entering the Crystal*,
but you enter the crystal with the specific intention of
receiving help with a problem. When inside the crystal you
ask for guidance, advice or a new perspective on an issue that
concerns you. This may be essentially practical or of a
spiritual nature, in which case you can use this method as a
regular focus for personal development. *Meeting the Wise
Teacher* will take you into the crystal and provide a sacred
place for meeting with your inner guide.

Exercise: Meeting the Wise Teacher

Sit upright and make sure you are warm, comfortable and relaxed. It is best to have your legs uncrossed with your feet placed flat on the ground or floor. Hold your crystal and allow yourself to become quiet and receptive, breathing regularly and slowly.

With thoughts of pure love and light ask your crystal to open an area of its structure so you may enter its perfect form.

See your crystal make a special space for you.

Enter your crystal through the doorway of light provided for you.

Feeling in a state of perfect balance, you choose to explore the interior of your crystal.

Allow all your senses to be open to experience your crystal.

Touch its sides, its foundation, with your face, your hands.

Allow your body to lean against a crystal wall.

Listen to any sounds you may hear.

Feel you are at home and totally welcomed by your crystal.

Now ask your wise teacher to appear to you.

Become aware of a shining figure approaching.

You can feel the energy of pure love radiating from this figure.

You know it is your guide or wise teacher.

Find a place where you can sit together and enjoy this sacred meeting.

Enjoy the attunement with this being that knows and loves you completely.

Share the heartfelt matters of your soul *(several minutes)*.

Now, bid farewell, knowing you will meet again many
times.
Indeed, you are never really apart.
Prepare to leave.
Thank your crystal for providing this sacred meeting place.
Re-focus on your breathing, wiggle your hands and feet
and return to the present.
Open your eyes.

4. ABSENT HEALING

Absent healing works by focusing your concentration and
prayer, linking your personal energy and will to divine consciousness, for the benefit of others. Although the recipient
is not present, distance is no impediment to the effectiveness
of absent healing. You might consider adding a form of
absent healing to the end of your personal meditations. By
sending out the energy that has built up during meditation as
love and light to the world, you will be adding to a vast pool
of good will available to those in need.

You can use crystals to enhance absent healing, outside of
specific meditation times, by placing the name or photo of
the person you wish to receive healing on a little table or altar
kept specifically for the purpose. Dedicate six little quartz
points or rose quartz crystals to the sacred work of bringing
perfect balance and harmony for healing as you arrange a six
pointed Star of David grid around the name or photo.

A note about absent healing — It is ethical, and good
manners, to ask the person beforehand if they would like to
receive healing, assuming they haven't already asked you for
it. It is my belief that we do not have the right to impose our
personal will or wishes on another in this way without their

permission — we can rarely be sure of the right outcome of any situation for ourselves, let alone for another person. While we all impose our wishes unconsciously a lot of the time, which is bad enough, to do so consciously carries a greater responsibility. There are rare occasions, perhaps if the person is unconscious, when it is not possible to ask their permission to give healing. In these circumstances you could meditate on the situation, asking that God's will be done or that your will becomes aligned with the higher self of the person concerned for their greatest good.

CHAPTER **18**

Crystals, Visualisation and Inner Journeys

Our real journey in life is interior.
Thomas Merton

There are some very useful self-help techniques which take the form of guided or scripted meditation exercises which make use of the creative imagination — with the specific intention of making changes in your life. Usually referred to as creative visualisation, this is a powerful technique which can definitely enhance personal development. Not everyone has a very developed visual imagination, but like a regularly exercised muscle, you will find that practice brings results. But it is not only the visual imagination that is important — the development of all the imaginal senses greatly enhances this type of meditation. Try the following mini-exercise to sharpen your awareness:

The Lemon Effect
Close your eyes.
Imagine you are holding a large, bright yellow, juicy lemon.
Really sense it!
Feel the texture of the peel
and smell its fresh tang.
Now see yourself cutting the lemon in half.

See the shiny, juicy flesh.
See the juice spray out.
Now cut it into quarters.
Can you smell it?
Really imagine it vividly.
Now pick up a segment of the lemon and suck it!

If you have done this you will probably have just discovered proof that your imagination affects you literally and physically.

Because imagination is so often denigrated as '*only* imagination', especially in childhood, its importance is often overlooked or dismissed. Yet it is the very faculty that creates your reality, consciously or, more often, unconsciously. If you can train and develop your creative imagination, you will have access to the building blocks of your future.

Working with crystals will help you to enhance your imaginative skills. Begin with the exercise, *Entering the Crystal* (see page 186), to establish a deep connection with a particular crystal of your choice — a clear quartz natural point or prism is recommended — and then ask your crystal to become your guide and helper, holding it throughout your meditation and the exercises that follow. You will be amazed how quickly you develop vivid images with the help of your crystal.

Creative imagination is fuelled by will, so it is wise to meditate on your motives before creating what you want. As the saying goes, be careful what you wish for. You will almost certainly get it! Consider the following:

The Interview
I am going to a job interview after years off bringing up my family. I spend the days before the interview worrying

and imagining myself unable to cope, being too out of
touch and failing to create a good impression. I sleep
badly and all my usual competence and confidence has
disintegrated. I have imagined in advance that I have
been out of the workplace too long and I am not equal to
the situation. When the interview comes, I feel a cloud
hanging over me and I am tongue-tied. I know it is a
disaster. I am told very gently that perhaps I don't quite
have the experience they need and I have the confirm-
ation I expected which is: 'I knew it would turn out like
that because I'm no good.' My self-esteem goes down
another notch!

Now replay the same situation:
For the days before the interview I visualise myself
confidently. I consider that my maturity and experience
mean I can think on my feet and respond quickly to
unexpected situations. I am used to managing a family
and all that entails. I am a mediator. I imagine I am
competent and comfortable with the interview, and well
on top of the questions I am likely to be asked. I really
want this job and I imagine myself doing it well, looking
forward to learning new skills and liking my new work
colleagues. I see myself being happy and fulfilled.

I prepare myself well the night before and remind myself
that the interviewers are human beings: daughters and
sons and, most probably, wives, husbands and parents. We
have a lot in common! They won't want to waste *their*
time any more than I want to waste *mine*. They have
invited me on the strength of my application. I visualise
myself happy to meet new people, interested in them,

their company and what they have to say. I sleep well and find I can even quite look forward to the interview. I am delighted when they tell me that my maturity and experience are just what are needed for the job on offer. I get the job.

In the next exercises I will show how creative visualisation can be used for personal change. My thanks to Ian Graham, always a source of wisdom and joy, for the *Vesselling* exercise, which is one of my favourites. It is wonderfully effective in releasing unwanted and inappropriate burdens:

Exercise: Vesselling
All of us act as vessels, that is, we carry individuals' (mother/father), groups' (political/social) or national expectations, career patterns, ways we dress or speak, stereotypes or attitudes in our psyches. Therefore we act as vessels for them. Some you will be happy to carry, but others you may have simply outgrown or you may feel inhibit or limit you in some way. Spend a few moments identifying anything you are carrying that has become a burden you would like to release. Examples might be 'dutiful daughter', 'like father like son', 'fat and jolly', '*we* don't say that', 'not in *those* trousers!'

You will need a sheet of paper and a pen. Using your *wrong* hand, draw a simple image of your vessel — something like a cup or a chalice — in the centre of your page, not too big. Now write on it, still using your wrong hand, what you are vesselling at this time. Keep it simple, a few words at most. When you are ready, complete as follows:

Stand up.

Imagine you are standing in front of a lake of crystal clear healing water.

Pull your vessel from your solar plexus.

With clear intention empty it into the lake.

Watch the chemical change as the lake water transforms the contents of the vessel.

Now turn your back to the lake.

Do this physically by turning round and go to the fountain just behind you.

Fill your vessel from its pure spring.

Drink from it until you feel satisfied.

You notice that however much you drink your cup remains full.

When you have finished, place the brimming cup in your heart.

Releasing the Past (see below) is likewise especially useful in preparation for a life change or new beginning. I have used it in workshops at New Year's Eve.

Exercise: (Part 1) Releasing the Past

Consider any circumstances and elements of the **past** which are holding you back from being, at heart, what you want to be and preventing you from doing what you want to do.

List these things on a piece of paper (*allow time*).

Next, consider and make a list of **present** conditions and circumstances you would like to change.

Perhaps you are unhappy at work? in a relationship? without a relationship?

Perhaps you are restricted by circumstances.
Are you in debt, lonely, frustrated, neglected?
List them all.

Spend plenty of time making your list and, if you feel like it, create a painting or a collage of images from old magazines that best represents the feelings which arise from the things you have listed and which you wish to change and let go.

You will have the opportunity to let go of all these things in the bonfire, freeing you to begin to take charge of your own future.

Ideally, make a small bonfire outdoors. If this is not possible, you could use an indoor fireplace.

(Part 2) The Bonfire

Imagine that the bonfire is lit from your own inner light, remembering it also represents your divine source.

Circle the bonfire clockwise attuning yourself to the fire, cleansing yourself in the smoke and heat.

Read your list: the past circumstances which still affect you and hold you back,

the present circumstances you would like to change.

Let your mind dwell for a while on each

turning them over in your mind.

Then let them go.

Imagine them being lifted like a great burden from your shoulders.

Feel the relief and the lightness.

Let go of the past.

You cannot change it.

But you can break the chains that are binding your present.
Imagine the chains being cut and throw them down.
You are free.
Study your collage if you have made one.
Feel the pain and then let it go.
In facing it you have overcome the power it has over you.
Ask the fire to consume your past limitations
to free you of false beliefs that you may no longer be a victim of circumstances or outworn conditioning.
Ask that you now learn to choose the rest of your life consciously and become what you desire to be.

Now take each paper in turn and twist it into a loose taper which you burn individually.
Consider what the paper contains as you watch the fire consume it.

Now warm your hands gently and place both hands across your forehead.
Warm them again and place both hands on your heart.
Warm them again and place them on your solar plexus.

You have symbolised the bringing of the divine flame to your mind, your heart (your spirit) and your body.
The gift of freedom has been given and accepted.
Transfer some of the light from the bonfire to the light within you.

If you wish, write down your experiences.

INNER JOURNEYS

Creative visualisation can be used as a starting point for inner journey work, using the crystal as a doorway to another level of reality. This might be seen as a form of 'astral travelling'. The reason a quartz crystal provides such a wonderful doorway is because crystals have the same appearance and form on the physical level as they do on the inner levels. This is one of the reasons why crystals have been invaluable to shamans since earliest times for accessing the worlds of non-ordinary reality and travelling in the dreamtime.

Exercise: Entering the Dreamtime

Sit upright and make sure you are warm, comfortable and relaxed. It is best to have your legs uncrossed and your feet placed flat on the ground or floor. Hold your crystal and allow yourself to become quiet and receptive, breathing regularly and slowly.

With thoughts of pure love and light ask your crystal to open an area of its structure so you may enter its perfect form.

See your crystal make a special space for you.

Enter your crystal through the doorway of light provided for you.

Feeling in a state of perfect balance, you choose to explore the interior of your crystal.

Allow all your senses to be open to experience your crystal.

Touch its sides, its foundation, with your face, your hands.

Allow your body to lean against a crystal wall.

Listen to any sounds you may hear.

Feel you are at home and totally welcomed by your crystal.

When you are ready, look for a silvery pathway or sparkling stream of water.

Follow it until you reach a crystal cave.

Go through the cave and emerge into a completely new and beautiful landscape.

Spend a little while exploring this new world (*several minutes*).

Now, prepare to return to your crystal cave.

Do not bring anything back with you from this otherworld journey.

Re-experience the interior of the crystal.

When you feel settled and centred, prepare to leave.

Thank your crystal for sharing its energies with you.

Re-focus on your breathing, wiggle your hands and feet and return to the present.

Open your eyes.

The reason for the instruction not to bring anything out with you from the otherworld (non-ordinary reality) is that it can create a link with the astral world which may sometimes give rise to troublesome intrusions into your everyday life.

CHAPTER 19

Meditation with Sound and Movement

If you wish to know the divine,
Feel the wind on your face and the warm sun
on your hand.

The Buddha

I have devoted this chapter to some moving meditations
that can be used with crystals, as they are a little different
from the other forms of meditation described in this
Section. Moving meditation exists in many traditions and
cultures across the world. Some of the most ancient forms
involve dancing in circles, whether it be the dances of the
native American, European folk dances or the mystical
whirling dances of the Sufis. What has come to the West as
the Chinese and Japanese martial arts traditions, especially
t'ai ch'i and *ch'i kung*, are also forms of moving meditation,
and to practise them properly involves an awareness that
does not separate the practitioner from the practice or from
the oneness and flow of life.

The effect of many mystical dances is to produce trance
and altered states of consciousness, often assisted by drumming or music and singing. Chanting can also be involved,
with or without movement. Drumming and chanting are
both primary tools in shamanic practice. Both have specific
effects on the mind and should be learned with the help of
an experienced practitioner.

SOUND VIBRATIONS

Just like light frequencies, radio waves and electromagnetic waves, sound is a vibrationary energy in the universe made up of invisible waves. These waves are measured in hertz (Hz) cycles per second, known as frequencies. Therefore a string that vibrates five hundred times in a second creates a sound that is measured as 500 Hz, the frequency of that particular sound. Human hearing is limited to a range of between 16 and 25,000 Hz, but animals hear different ranges — dogs, dolphins and bats, for example, hear sounds in the high hertz that are undetectable to us. At certain levels we refer to a range as ultrasound.

While our hearing is limited, we resonate to sounds much deeper and much higher than we can detect, due to the harmonics that are produced from a particular sound. Harmonics are the other notes produced at the same time and in mathematical ratio to the fundamental note. So the first harmonic vibrates at a rate twice as fast as the original note; the second harmonic is three times faster, and so on. The vibrations of the earth, or the stars, may be way below our audible range but, multiplied up, they are harmonically resonant to a range we can hear. A healthy organ in your body will vibrate at a frequency that resonates harmoniously with the rest of your body; but if it is diseased, a different resonance is introduced which will upset the harmony of the body. And so it is within the environment. Thus your own body frequencies, heard or not, influence and are influenced by universal frequencies. Atoms and stars are sonically interactive.

CHANTING

Chanting is seen by many as a primary meditation tool as well as a fundamental of religious practice, notably the Gregorian chants of the monastic Christian Church and the mantra of the East — among the most famous being the 'OM'. Chant used as a mantra is a sound, a word, or a group of words, which is repeated so often that the person who is sounding them is put in touch with the atmosphere which the word represents.

This works in two ways — firstly by association with the meaning of the word and the suggestion it places in your mind, and then by the harmonic resonance of the sound itself. Some sounds, for example, are harsh whereas others are soothing. Many sacred words come from Hebrew and Sanskrit, where not only do the words represent something sacred but the sound of the word carries the same meaning as a sacred resonance — its seed or essence. The Yoga Sutras of Patanjaii state:

> *Through the sounding of the Word AUM and through reflection upon its meaning, the Way is found.*
> *From this comes the realisation of the Inner Self and the removal of all obstacles.*

The sacred word OM or AUM (pronounce the word in the way that seems best to you) from the Sanskrit, is a universal mantra. William Bloom in his *Meditation in a Changing World* says: 'AUM has a note to it which is slightly more "earthed" and incarnated than OM.' But he also notes you may find during chanting that your AUM will run into OM and the other way round. He goes on to explain that while the meaning of OM has no exact translation, it can be expressed in terms of divine breath, breathing into life the essence of divine mind — literally 'In the beginning was the Word.' To begin, there is the out-breath — before any sound is heard —

and this represents the very beginning of creation in divine mind. There follows a long vowel sound representing the breath of creation moving through space in order to bring divine thought into manifestation. Lastly this manifestation is vibrated into form through the sounding of the consonant at the end.

A mantra can be sounded out loud or silently in your imagination — sound it as often as feels comfortable. Make the sound clearly and confidently and then relax and be open and attentive to any changes the sound has stimulated. Repetition and attention will eventually bring palpable effects to your energy. Try chanting through your favourite quartz — the effects are powerful and exhilarating. Don't overdo it when you start out — a little regular daily practice is best — so that increased understanding of the effects comes through gentle experience.

You can make up your own mantra, or choose a mantra to suit your needs, for example, 'All is One' or Mother Julian of Norwich's 'All is Well and All shall be Well.' The Beatles' mantra 'All you need is love — love is all you need' is also very effective. Or you can make up a mantra to suit your particular needs of the moment. As with affirmations, a clear intention and repetition will bring success by aligning you with the resonance and inner meaning of your word or phrase.

As we know that crystals can convert sound frequencies into light and that the human body contains crystalline structures, such as our bones and the crystal-colloidal structure of the brain, it is not unreasonable to suppose that this is what causes sounds to change when chanting and that what takes place in the body, that is, vibrating certain sounds, can have a transformational effect on the whole energy system. Overtone chanting originally comes from Tibet where it is part of monastic discipline. It has very profound effects on the energy system, either cleansing and wonderful or unbalancing and disturbing, depending on the quality of the practice and the degree of reliable guidance available. Among my clients I have seen several casualties from overtone chanting workshops who have found afterwards that they were prey to anxiety, intrusive dreams and visions as a result of being opened up psychically and energetically, perhaps before they were ready, without the guidance or support to help them understand and control what had happened. If you are interested in learning overtone chanting — and the rewards can be extraordinary — you will not be surprised that I recommend you find yourself a good teacher.

MOVING CRYSTALS

Carry crystals, a clear quartz point in each hand (as described on page 55), as you do the following exercise, and become conscious of the crystals vibrating with light and energy as you go. It is a valuable exercise in its own right, especially performed outdoors, but it is also useful to use in preparation for the *Sacred Spiral Walk*, described below.

Treading the Light

Imagine the streaming light that is your core energy
flowing down your spine
flowing down your legs to the soles of your feet.
Breathe the light down to your feet for a few minutes.
Gradually become aware that wherever you step
you are sending light through your feet into the ground.
This will set up a resonance.
You will begin to feel energy travelling up from the earth
through the soles of your feet in response.

Thus a beautiful two-way flow begins
and you start to tread consciously
de-lighting in and a-lighting on the ground.
With every step you bless
and receive the rich blessing of the earth as you go.

This exercise can be, quite literally, so moving that you may
begin to sense the rhythm of the earth and dance along the
sacred songs that reach you through your feet. This deep
rhythm of life is beautifully expressed in the following song
of Uvavnuk, an Eskimo woman shaman, recorded by Natalie
Curtis in *The Indian's Book*.

The Song of Uvavnuk
*The great sea
Has sent me adrift.
It moves me
As the weed in a great river.
Earth and the great weather
Move me
Have carried me away
And move my inward parts with joy.*

Perhaps we too can learn to make our whole lives a joyful
meditation.

SPIRALS OF TRANSFORMATION
The spiral layout is a wonderful basis for a moving meditation
and is best used outside or in a room where there is enough
space for you to walk the spiral comfortably, with a chair
(place the centre crystal point upwards beneath) or cushion
(sit cross-legged, with the centre crystal held in both hands in

your lap, point upwards) at the centre. The *Crystal Spiral Maze* (described in Chapter 15, page 166) is ideal for this meditation. To make your spiral you should follow the instructions and diagram given there.

Take care with this meditation as the spiral form is very powerful and will quite radically alter your perceptions. As you move along the pathway to the centre, you seem to travel a vast distance and lose all sense of time. It is really helpful to do this meditation with a partner and guide. They can read the text of the meditation, pacing it with your walk, so that you reach the centre at the time indicated in the meditation. The walk will be further enhanced if you close your eyes or wear a blindfold and allow yourself to be guided through the spiral by your partner.

When you reach the centre you will *become* the meeting node of the upper and lower worlds and the eye which sees through to other realms of reality. If you are blindfolded, remove the blindfold and open your eyes at the centre. When you are ready, make your way out of the spiral clockwise, bringing the wisdom you have contacted with you back to the world.

Sacred Spiral Walk
Energy flows in spirals, circular and wave-like: like the tides of life
the sea
the moon
the seasons
ebb and flow.
All are born, expand, contract, re-form
active and passive by turns.

The spiral becomes also the double spiral of your own
DNA
as you move to the centre
and out again with a new awareness.

As you move very slowly and deliberately, anticlockwise
through the spiral, the world begins to dissolve.
And you are at the centre.
Take your seat at the heart of creation, where all worlds
meet
and all is one time
no time
here.
And nowhere — which is to say you are *now here*.
You are at the centre of creation
the eye of the whirlwind
the centre of a spinning galaxy of shining stars
the tiny spiral shell
where all possibility is born.
Be here now (*allow several minutes*)
until you make your return
out to the place where you started, but seeing as if for the
first time
from a new perspective,
reborn!

Always take time at the end of a meditation to return gently
to ordinary reality. Begin by focusing on your breathing and
take some quiet time to process your experiences.

Colour Crystal Directory

Most crystal directories are listed alphabetically, which makes them useless for identifying an unknown stone. (You need to know the name before you can look it up.) In an ingenious break with tradition, this directory is organised by *colour*. This means you know at once which section to consult simply by looking at the colour of the crystal in your hand. All the crystals referred to in the book are listed under the appropriate colour group and a brief description is given of each one along with its basic uses in the home, workplace and garden. Because light and colour, as manifested by crystals, are fundamental keys to energetic healing, stones within the same colour category often have broadly similar effects.

WHAT ARE CRYSTALS?

Crystals are blossoms from the very heart and fabric of our planet. Out of the debris and white-hot gases of star-stuff which condensed to form the earth hundreds of millions of years ago, elements and compounds were formed which settled into layers: a hard outer crust, a semi-liquid mantle and a molten core. Deep within the newly formed earth, mysterious beauty manifested — crystals began to grow in the different environments formed within the planet's structure. Precisely how they were formed is still pretty much a mystery, but we do know that life depends on the earth's minerals. We know some crystals even come from deep within the earth's semi-liquid mantle and are thrown up by volcanic activity; others are formed inside the rock, often in open pockets or in long seams; while still more are formed on the earth's surface.

But their true beauty remains hidden without the presence of light. The fascinating way crystals interact with light causes the wonderful ranges of colour, brilliance, luminosity, intensity and fire so apparent in stones such as rubies, diamonds, lapis lazuli, moonstones, opals and quartz, jewels prized throughout the ages for their strange power and awesome beauty.

Silicon is by far the most common of the surface elements, making up a large proportion of the crust of the planet, where it combines easily with oxygen to make silicon dioxide, otherwise known as quartz. Silicon dioxide, in varying proportions, provides the vast majority of our mineral compounds and it is widely distributed throughout the planet — just imagine that whenever you relax on the beach, you are lying on millions of tiny grains of quartz crystal, coloured gold by iron in the sea water.

Minerals have a chemical composition and a regular internal atomic structure which gives them constant, or almost constant, physical properties. It doesn't matter how vast or how minutely they are ground; each piece of a particular crystal displays the same structure and properties. Minerals are identified by measuring properties such as density and refraction. Crystals are classified into specific groups by measuring their relative hardness, specific gravity and by observing their internal symmetry.

HARDNESS

A crystal's hardness depends on how strongly the atoms are held together. A scale of hardness relating to all minerals was devised in 1812 by an Austrian, Freidrich Mohs, and is known as Mohs' Scale. Taking ten minerals as standards, he arranged them in order of hardness so that one mineral could only scratch those below it on the scale. The scale goes from 1 to 10, based on talc as the softest (1), gypsum (2), calcite (3), fluorite (4), apatite (5), orthoclase (6), quartz (7), topaz (8), corundum (9) and diamond as the hardest (10). This is a relative scale and it does not mean that diamond is ten times as hard as talc: it is, in fact, many more times harder.

SPECIFIC GRAVITY

The specific gravity, or relative density, of a crystal reflects the way the atoms are packed together. It is defined as the weight per unit volume (a crystal's weight compared to that of an equal volume of distilled water). To calculate specific gravity (SG), take the weight of the crystal in air (W^1) and its weight in water (W^2). W^1 divided by W^1 *minus* W^2 gives you the specific gravity.

CRYSTAL SYSTEMS

Crystal systems refer to symmetry, which depends on a crystal's internal structure and the arrangement of atoms within it. If a crystal can be divided so that each half is the mirror image of the other, the dividing line is called the plane of symmetry.

Isometric

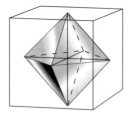

Orthorhombic

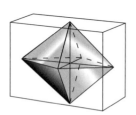

Tetragonal

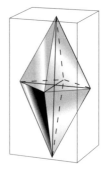

Monoclinic

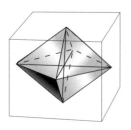

Hexagonal

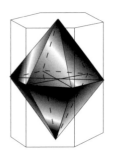

Triclinic

The six crystal systems

There are seven main classifications:

Cubic (having the greatest symmetry)
Three axes of the same length and at right angles to each other.

Tetragonal
Three axes at right angles to each other, two on the same plane of equal length. The third is perpendicular to them. Four or eight sided prisms and pyramid shapes.

Hexagonal
Three of the four axes are in a single plane radiating equally from the centre. The fourth axis is perpendicular to, and a different length from, the others. Six sided shapes.

Tribunal
Similar to hexagonal. Parallel to the long axis, there are three planes of symmetry.

Orthorhombic
Three unequal axes at right angles to one other. Shapes include variations on the pyramid form.

Monoclinic
Prism has inclined top and bottom faces. Three unequal axes, two at right angles to each other and the third at an incline to the other plane. Shapes are prism like.

Triclinic
Three unequal axes all at different angles to each other. Three pairs of faces. Shapes with much less symmetry than shown in other six crystal systems.

BLACK STONES
Tourmaline
Hardness: 7, Specific Gravity: 2.9–3.2, Crystal System: Hexagonal

Fine tourmaline is found in Austria, Yugoslavia, the Urals, Norway, Elba, Madagascar, Mozambique, Sri Lanka, Burma, Nepal, Brazil, Australia and the USA. It is most commonly a very dark blue-green or black (this type is known as **schorlite**). It can also be pink, red, orange, green and colourless. The crystals usually occur as elongated prismatic columns, usually in granites or pegmatites, and are often zoned in different colours — green at the outside to pink or red at the centre is known as 'watermelon' tourmaline, which is often sliced and polished. When heated or rubbed, tourmaline produces a distinctive positive and negative electromagnetic charge.

Home: Protects against background radiation. Strengthening and vitalising properties are helpful in calming the nerves and dispelling fears. This crystal is a powerful healer and will regulate the hormones as well as ease blood poisoning and infectious diseases. It enhances the crystalline properties of the body, balances the subtle bodies and is strongly protective, encouraging restful sleep. **Watermelon tourmaline** is also good for balancing the endocrine system and metabolism and will help to strengthen the immune system.

Work: Helps to improve concentration, balances energies and protects against background radiation from electrical equipment. Helpful if worn when using a cellular phone.

Garden: Tourmaline (especially green) strengthens the life force of plants — make gem water and spray or water new plants to help them to establish well. Useful too when moving plants to a new site.

Elixir: Excellent for treating negative conditions caused by geopathic stress and background radiation.

Hematite

Hardness: 5½-6½, Specific Gravity: 4.9-5.3, Crystal System: Hexagonal

Hematite is a fairly common hydrothermal mineral which forms under oxidising conditions in igneous rock as well as in many sedimentary rocks. Major sources of hematite are Canada, the USA, Brazil, Russia and Angola, but many European countries also produce fine crystals. A principal source of iron ore, this heavy black, iron grey or reddish crystal has a strong metallic lustre and is vivid red (hence the name) when powdered. It is also used in polishes and as a pigment.

Home: Energising and grounding, it is good for the circulation of oxygen in the blood. The ancient Egyptians used hematite to treat inflammations, haemorrhages and hysteria. Galen used it for inflamed eyelids and headaches and Pliny for blood and bilious disorders, burns and for healing wounds. Hematite will bring helpful confidence to children and will promote restful sleep.

Work: It strengthens the will, personal courage and optimism. Very helpful for grounding — making inspiration a physical reality. Brings mental clarity and focus to any tasks and especially helpful when studying. Carry a pocket tumble for stress resistance, to ease anxiety or to overcome jet-lag.

Garden: Brings strength and energy to weak and ailing plants.

Elixir: Treats low vitality and low self-esteem.

Obsidian (and snowflake obsidian)

A volcanic glass rather than a crystal but has certain useful properties. Screens negativity and grounds chaotic energies.

Polished black obsidian makes a wonderful scrying tool for psychics while simultaneously acting as a protection against negative influences.

Home: A friendly influence, obsidian absorbs anger and criticism and eases tense atmospheres. Improves hearing and (snowflake obsidian) clairaudience. **Snowflake obsidian** balances out extreme attitudes and brings greater acceptance of the 'shadow' side of the self, and clears old blocks. **Apache tear**, a form of obsidian pebble found with small tear-shaped markings on the surface, is helpful in times of sorrow, bringing an atmosphere in which it is safe to grieve.

Work: Protective to those exposed to physical danger. Promotes personal clarity by honest reflection and an awareness of the changes that may be needed in order to remove flaws.

Elixir: Add to bath water for a soothing energy and smooth skin.

Smoky quartz

A member of the quartz family (see entry for clear quartz), smoky quartz is smoky grey or dark brown due to natural radiation (although a lot that comes from the USA is artificially radiated to almost black). It is slightly more grounding than clear quartz and usually available in natural points, as well as tumblestones, polished prisms, spheres and polished shapes.

Home: Increases fertility and balances sexual energy. Useful for clearing subconscious blocks and negativity at all levels, it is mildly sedative and good for easing depression. Atomise with gem water to cleanse the environment of negative influences.

Work: Protects against background radiation and encourages balance in all aspects of work, maintaining optimism and clarity.

Garden: Used as a gem water spray, smoky quartz is cleansing and protective to all plants.

Elixir: Generally strengthening. Enhances the effectiveness of other gem elixirs. Use as atomiser to cleanse the aura.

RED, ORANGE AND PEACH STONES
Agate (Quartz group)
Hardness: 6½–7, Specific Gravity: 2.6, Crystal System: Hexagonal

Most important deposits are found in India, Brazil and Uruguay, but it is also found in quantity in the USA, Canada, Germany and Russia. A banded microcrystalline quartz variety of chalcedony, agate occurs in many varieties and is often dyed for decorative purposes.

Home: Often called the '**fire stone**', agate imparts a sense of strength and courage. It is a powerful healer, helping the digestion, lymph system, circulation and pulses. It is earthing and energetic.

Garden: Use **moss agate** as a spray to assist plant care and growth.

Elixir: **Fire agate** is helpful for courage and discrimination especially in practical and material concerns. Moss agate will strengthen a connection with nature.

Carnelian (Quartz group)
Hardness: 6½–7, Specific Gravity: 2.58–2.64, Crystal System: Hexagonal

Carnelian is a brownish-orange to red form of chalcedony found in India, Madagascar, Brazil and Uruguay. A microcrystalline variety of quartz, it usually forms fibrous masses. Natural crystals are without layering or banding but, because they are porous, they can be dyed.

Home: Aids tissue regeneration and supports the functions of the kidneys, liver, lungs, pancreas and gall bladder. Eases menstrual cramps and the pain of gout and arthritis. Improves appetite and overall vitality. Carnelian is warming and energises the physical, emotional and mental bodies.

Work: Brings energy, confidence, boldness and assertiveness.

Garden: Carnelian strongly connects with the fertility of the earth and brings support and strength. Helps the gardener with allergies such as hay fever if worn or taken as elixir.

Elixir: Eases melancholy and touchiness. Brings objectivity and enthusiasm.

Copper

Hardness: 2½–3, Specific Gravity: 8.93–9, Crystal System: Cubic

Mostly mined around the Great Lakes of Canada, in the USA, UK, Russia, Australia, Mexico, Peru, Chile, Sweden, Germany and Zimbabwe, copper is important in modern electrical engineering. A valuable metal for centuries, it usually occurs in branches but occasionally as crystals. Coppery-red when first broken, it tarnishes to dull brown. It is soluble in nitric acid and is very malleable. Energise in the sun.

Home: In healing, copper can be used as a strong conductor of energy and it is effective in treating inflammatory conditions such as rheumatism and arthritis (copper bracelets are commonly available). Useful to strengthen general energy, the metabolism and blood flow. Copper is a very useful detoxifier worn next to the skin.

Work: Improves general energy levels, confidence and self-esteem. Can antidote the effects of microwave radiation.

Garden: Among the important trace elements, copper is needed in small amounts to ensure healthy plant growth, although in healthy soil a deficiency is rare. Copper-based sprays are effective in controlling fungal leaf spots. *Elixir*: Use as a gem water in a poultice to draw out infection in wounds.

Garnet (Garnet group)

The more common garnets are named and are distinguished by colour and other features.

Hardness: 6½–7½, Specific Gravity: 3.5–4.3, Crystal System: Cubic

Widespread across the world, fine examples of garnets come from Switzerland, Austria, Germany, Czechoslovakia, Italy, Russia, Finland, the USA, Canada, Mexico, Australia, Greenland, Tanzania and Kenya. Trapezoid and rhomboid garnet crystals are common as well as massive and granular formations. **Rhodolite** is the most valuable of the red garnets and can vary in colour from rose red to pale violet. **Pyrope** (from the Greek *pyropos* meaning fiery) is the deep red variety of garnet and a semi-precious gemstone. **Almandine** is dark brownish-red or purple-black and is occasionally cut into gemstones if very brightly coloured and clear. **Spessartine** is yellowish-orange to red-brown and gem quality stones are rare. **Grossular** crystals of green or yellow tint are often cut as gemstones. Other forms include **andradite** and the uncommon **uvarovite**.

Home: Good for strengthening the heart, thyroid, liver and kidneys, the spessartine variety is especially good for various types of anaemia. It has long been associated with passion, balancing the sex drive and the forces of the *kundalini*. Spiritualising and uplifting.

Work: Improves interpersonal relationships. Brings warmth, understanding and commitment to others, ideas and projects and to oneself. Enhances the creative imagination and can bring changes of direction, expansion or inspiration at lightning speed.

Elixir: Eases nausea during detoxification. Builds health, eliminating negative influences within the aura.

Jasper (Quartz group)
Hardness: 6½-7, Specific Gravity: 2.6-2.9, Crystal System: Hexagonal
Named from the Greek *iaspis*, the 'spotted stone', after the spotting on the green variety (see Bloodstone), jasper is a form of chalcedony. It is found world-wide although famous deposits are found in Germany, France, India, Russia and the USA. Single-coloured jaspers are rare and the range of colours varies widely, but they are often red-brown. A yellow form is found in Mexico and the USA.

Home: Strengthens the physical body, especially the liver, bladder and gall bladder. Associated with the element of earth, it is physically and emotionally balancing and grounding. Boosts depleted energy resulting from illness. Children benefit from this stone for its nurturing and comforting qualities. Assists dream recall.

Work: Great for promoting business success and increases of all kinds. Worn by shamans as a protection against negative influences and for its powerful sun connection. Sacred in the native American tradition and honoured for its help and protection whilst travelling (physically and astrally). Brings fresh ideas and inspires new and effective strategies.

Elixir: Helps those suffering from nightmares and disturbed dream states.

Rhodochrosite (Calcite group)

Hardness: 3½–4½, Specific Gravity: 3.3–3.7, Crystal System: Hexagonal

Sometimes known as '**Inca-rose**' because it is found in stalactite formations in abandoned Inca silvermines, rhodochrosite is usually pale pink to deep rose-red in colour. Fairly widely distributed, with fine crystals found in Colorado (USA), Mexico, Argentina, South Africa, Namibia, Romania, Spain, Italy and Germany, it usually occurs in hydrothermal veins and sedimentary rock in massive or granular form but occasionally as rhombohedral crystals with curved faces. The name is from the Greek *rhodon* meaning 'rose' and *chros* 'colour'. In large quantities it is a source for manganese. Rhodochrosite is also used to make decorative objects and beads.

Home: Rhodochrosite helps with emotional trauma and mental breakdown, increasing qualities of courage and will power. Good for improving eyesight, treating spleen, kidney, heart and blood circulation, it also assists memory and aligns the subtle bodies. Rhodochrosite balances passion with love, linking the solar plexus and the heart, and enhances self-esteem, love and acceptance. Helpful when working with trauma, healing the inner child and issues of shame, loss, fear and abandonment.

Work: For self-esteem and confidence. Inspires beneficial changes to old routines and new ways of seeing and self-expression.

Garden: The pH (ranging between 1–14) of the soil affects the solubility of minerals and hence their availability to plants — an acid soil (below 7) often has an excess of manganese, whereas an alkaline soil (higher than 7) is often deficient. While the pH of the soil is generally controlled by the calcium level, an alkaline soil would benefit from a rhodochrosite gem water spray.

Elixir: For emotional exhaustion, panic and frustration.

Ruby (Corundum group)

Hardness: 9, Specific Gravity: 3.9–4.1, Crystal System: Hexagonal Found in Burma, Afghanistan, India, Pakistan, Sri Lanka, Thailand, Africa, the USA and China, rubies tend to occur in marble-like rocks, in some intermediate rocks and pegmatites. Rubies and sapphires are different colours of corundum, the crystalline form of aluminium oxide. Rubies, the red corundum, are much rarer than sapphires and have long been prized as the most precious coloured gemstones. Large gem-quality rubies are 30 to 50 times rarer than diamonds.

Rubies are extremely hard — low-quality crystals are powdered and used for highly specialised cutting and polishing. Chrome causes their red colouring which is often uneven in tone within the same deposit. They become darker when exposed to natural light and sometimes have tiny rutile inclusions, giving the stones a silky appearance, which reflects light and can cause a six pointed star effect. These rubies are cut as cabochons to show off the stars to perfection. Heat treatment is very commonly used to enhance the clarity and colour. Ruby is considered to be the prince of gems, always associated with leadership and authority.

Home: Traditionally used to preserve the body and improve the mind. It strengthens the blood, the heart and immunity. It stimulates and invigorates the entire physical and mental system.

Workplace: Ruby brings qualities of courage and integrity to leadership and power. Increases stamina, stimulates creativity and mental powers.

Garden: Because of its aluminium content, alkaline soils would benefit from a ruby gem water spray.

Elixir: Balances heart *chakra* and amplifies energy of divine love. Helps those dealing with distress around the father relationship. Stops procrastination, bringing focus and confidence.

YELLOW AND GOLD STONES
Gold
Hardness: 2½, Specific Gravity: 15.5-19.3, depending on purity, Crystal System: Cubic
The main gold producers in the world are South Africa and the USA. Also mined in Australia, India, Brazil, Bolivia, Mexico, Austria, Russia, Canada and Papua New Guinea. Sources in the UK include north Wales, Cornwall, East Sutherland and Leadhills, south Scotland. A soft, non-tarnishing, rare yellow metal which can occur in crystal form, gold has been precious to mankind since earliest recorded history. The 'sweat of the sun' of the Incas has, during the past millennium, become the principal way of storing wealth. Because of its ability to conduct heat and electricity without tarnishing, it is widely used in technology. It has a very high specific gravity and is insoluble in single acids.
Home and Workplace: Gold is master healer. It attracts positive energy into the aura, balances the hemispheres of the brain, strengthens the nervous system, aids tissue regeneration and cleanses and energises the entire physical body. It amplifies thought forms and personal illumination.

Citrine (Quartz group)
Hardness: 7, Specific Gravity: 2.6, Crystal System: Hexagonal
A rare, golden yellow form of quartz found in Brazil, Madagascar, the USA, France and Russia. Heat-treated amethyst and smoky quartz is often sold as citrine. This 'drop of

sunlight' brings hope and lifts the spirits. It raises self-esteem and enhances self-healing. Citrine attracts abundance and a sense of confidence in the positive outcome of enterprises and events. It is usually available as natural points or clusters and as tumblestones.

Home: Citrine brings warmth and prosperity into the home. Use in living areas — the family room, playroom, kitchen/dining-room. Outgoing and sociable. Associated with luck and money. Helpful in overcoming lack of confidence, depression or over-sensitivity to the opinion of others.

Work: Brings inspiration, success, confidence, courage and prosperity at work. Especially good to carry or wear for public speaking, presentations, examinations, competitive sports or for the launch of new business/products/ideas. Attracts wealth. Especially helpful for careers in advertising, the arts and media, sales and marketing.

Garden: Brings energy and light. Useful in lifting stagnant energy in dark or enclosed places. Citrine gem water brings extra brightness to all yellow-leafed and petalled plants and any that need an energy boost. Citrine is a good choice for a sociable or lively section of the garden such as the patio, barbecue or play area.

Elixir: Uplifting and improves self-esteem. Will aid poor digestion. Good in combination with other elixirs as it improves receptivity and brings confidence to make changes.

Gold Tiger Eye (Quartz group)
Hardness: 7, Specific Gravity: 2.6, Crystal System: Hexagonal (but microcrystalline)
A banded chalcedony quartz formed with crocidolite fibres which give its characteristic sheen. Found in South Africa, Western Australia, Burma, India and the USA. The distinctive

stripes are golden to brown, caused by the brown iron content, against a nearly black ground.

Home: Good for the whole digestive system, the pancreas, liver, stomach, spleen and colon. Tiger's eye helps deal with 'butterflies in the tummy', bringing courage while softening stubborn pride.

Work: Brings strength and flexibility, enhances self-knowledge and clear sightedness, balances and grounds personal power, turning ideas into reality.

Elixir: Treats 'stage fright' and fear of success as well as failure.

Topaz

Hardness: 8, Specific Gravity: 3.6, Crystal System: Orthorhombic

Found in Germany, Italy, Japan, Afghanistan, Burma, Africa, the USA, Ukraine and Russia, the main source of Topaz is found in Minas Gerais in Brazil where crystals of up to 270 kg have been found. These hard prismatic, granular or massive crystals are formed in pegmatites from very highly compressed magma. *Topas* means 'heat' or 'fire' in Sanskrit. A fine gemstone, true topaz is a light to golden yellow, but there are three other varieties, pink, blue and colourless. Many colourless topazes are irradiated to make them blue, and yellowish stones can be heat-treated to turn them pink.

Home:Topaz brings the strength to deal with the trials in life. It balances the emotions and calms the temper. It warms and awakens, bringing hopefulness and radiance. It strengthens and regenerates the cell tissues and is an excellent detoxifier. It is also good for the thyroid, metabolism and digestive organs.

Work: Controls temper and over-reaction in adversity. Excellent for artists, musicians and writers, this soothing

stone assists all forms of creativity in harmony with the higher self.
Elixir: For anger, jealousy, worry and depression. Stabilises emotions and calms passions.

GREEN STONES
Apophyllite
Occurring as pseudo-cubic crystals, natural pyramidal structures and granular masses, the finest white, green and clear crystals are found in Poona, India.
Home: Bridges the physical and spiritual dimensions, helping to understand the underlying meaning in physical conditions. Excellent for inner journeys, lucid dreaming and astral travel, enabling full consciousness during the experiences. Facilitates direct access to higher self and channelled information. **Green apophyllite** energises the heart and allows a perfect flow of life force through the *chakras*, bringing joy and laughter.
Work: Stimulates intuition, reflection and self-knowledge. Brings light-hearted wisdom in relation to problems.
Garden: Revitalising. Useful as gem water for plants that have suffered from drought or very poor soil conditions.
Elixir: Brings light, energy and love. Use to charge or energise self, objects and other stones.

Aventurine (Quartz group)
Hardness: 7, Specific Gravity: 2.63–2.65, Crystal System: Hexagonal
A variety of crystalline quartz with sparkling mica inclusions found in Brazil, Australia, India, Nepal and Russia. The name is from the Italian *avventura*, meaning 'chance', due to the accidental discovery of a spangled glass.

Home: In ancient Tibet aventurine was used for near-sightedness. Centring, soothing and tranquillising. Purifies the subtle bodies, strengthens blood and improves elasticity of muscle tissue. Effective in treating skin diseases. Brings love and delight to the heart, easing fears and anxiety.
Work: Eases emotional stress when under pressure. Good for exam nerves. Adds an additional element of good luck in all undertakings.
Garden: Healing and light giving. Brings a strong connection with Mother Earth and a sparkle of joy that will inspire the gardener. A few aventurine tumblestones near a garden seat bring peace and happiness.
Elixir: For fearfulness. Useful in treating psychosomatic illness and in psychotherapy for helping to release past trauma.

Amazonite (Feldspar group)
Hardness: 6–6½, Specific Gravity: 2.56–2.58, Crystal System: Triclinic
This feldspar mineral takes its name from the Amazon River from which it was believed the crystals flowed. Main deposits are found in Brazil, Australia, India, Russia, Madagascar, Namibia, Zimbabwe and the USA. Mostly light green, but sometimes bluish or blue-green, these squat crystals often have a mottled appearance and are semi-opaque.
Home: Like most of the green stones, amazonite is soothing to the nervous system. Amazonite aligns the heart and solar plexus *chakras*. It is good for balancing the subtle bodies and for assisting in letting go of harmful tendencies, giving freedom to creative expression. Encourages friendship and good relationships.
Work: For ease of communication and confidence in personal creativity, artistic expression and in healing work.

Elixir: Helps assimilation of the life force and enhances the effects of most other vibrational remedies.

Bloodstone (Quartz group)

Hardness: 6½-7, Specific Gravity: 2.58-2.64, Crystal System: Hexagonal

Dark green with spots of red, a microcrystalline variety of quartz which usually forms fibrous masses, bloodstone is a form of chalcedony found in India, Madagascar, Brazil and Uruguay. Also known as **heliotrope**. Highly electromagnetic due to iron content.

Home: A powerful physical healer, bloodstone oxygenates and strengthens the blood, the heart, spleen and bone marrow and assists in balancing iron deficiency. Good for menstrual problems and anaemia. Protective and energising to the whole system.

Work: Brings courage and friendship.

Elixir: Eases melancholy and touchiness. Brings objectivity and enthusiasm.

Jade

Hardness: 6½-7, Specific Gravity: 3.4, Crystal System: Monoclinic

Found in New Zealand (source of rare colours), China, Tibet, Burma, Japan, Guatemala and the USA. Jade was used for making prehistoric weapons and tools because it is hard to splinter. The name comes from the Spanish *piedra de ijada* meaning 'stone of the side' because it was believed jade cured kidney problems if placed on the side of the body.

Although often associated with the Orient, jade was valued more highly than gold in pre-Columban cultures and carries mystical associations to this day, despite good synthetics. Rarely found in crystal form and more commonly as large alluvial pebbles, it is usually green or greyish white, although it is occasionally found in blue-grey, lilac, yellow, orange, red or brown.

Home: In China, jade was used to increase longevity, strengthen the body and make men more fertile. Assists with childbirth and helps relieve eye disorders and to detoxify the system. Jade has a nurturing and peaceful quality, bringing healing and emotional balance.

Work: Brings realism, integrity and assists in ability to express true feelings. Confucius said jade was a reminder of the integrity of the mind and soul. It is associated with the five chief Chinese virtues of wisdom, courage, justice, mercy and modesty. A very good influence, especially if you are applying *feng shui* techniques in the workplace.

Elixir: Can be used to make a soothing wash for skin problems and as a strengthening hair rinse.

Dioptase

Hardness: 5, Specific Gravity: 3.3, Crystal System: Hexagonal

Bright emerald green dioptase crystals are found in West Africa, Chile, Russia and the USA. The crystals occur in the oxidised parts of copper veins. Popular with mineral collectors and jewellers, dioptase strengthens the central nervous and cardio-vascular systems and eases nervous stomachs, ulcers and blood pressure. Brings a sense of well-being, emotional stability and engenders abundance, prosperity, progress and health.

Home: A happy, stable energy for the home. Dioptase is calming and healing and suitable in most areas where these influences would be helpful.

Work: Brings abundance and prosperity into the work environment. Encourages progress and successful development of ideas and projects. Helpful for calming nervous stomachs and easing stressful conditions.

Emerald (Beryl group)
Hardness: 7½-8, Specific Gravity: 2.6-2.8, Crystal System: Hexagonal
Found in Colombia, India, Pakistan, Australia, Brazil, South Africa, Siberia, Tanzania, Zambia and Zimbabwe, emerald, the bright green variety of **beryl**, has always been valued as a precious stone. The deeper the colour, the higher its value. Emeralds, which are very hard and prismatic, occur as crystals in granites and pegmatites close to an area of rising magma. They are rarely transparent and usually contain inclusions due to heating cracks, liquid or gas bubbles or to the presence of other crystals. Synthetic emeralds are now being made with artificial inclusions to simulate natural ones! Emerald is associated with Venus.
Home: For growth, fertility and love. Vitalises and tones the body and mind and stimulates memory. It strengthens the heart, liver, kidneys and immune system. In the past emeralds were used to heal skin problems and they have a strong antiseptic reputation. They enhance dreams and meditation.
Work: Brings prosperity, kindness, tranquillity, patience and balance — all helpful in a work context.
Elixir: Amplifies qualities of kindness, patience and balance. Relieves hidden fears.

Malachite
Hardness: 3½-4, Specific Gravity: 3.75-4, Crystal System: Monoclinic
Malachite is a common copper mineral found extensively in the world. Large amounts have been found in Zaire, Zambia,

South Africa, Zimbabwe, Australia, Russia, the USA and Israel. A popular green gem with a vitreous lustre — the name comes from the Greek *maloche*, because of its likeness to the leaves of the mallow plant — malachite is used as an ornamental stone which, when polished, displays its distinctive banding. It is usually formed in the upper, oxidisation zone of copper deposits. The Rosicrucians believed malachite symbolised the rising of spiritual man.

Home:Traditionally malachite is used to strengthen the head, teeth, eyes, kidneys, pancreas, spleen and stomach. Also to promote sleep and increase fertility and lactation. Malachite was thought to protect the wearer from falling and avert faintness. This calming stone is a powerful healer and balancer to the physical and emotional system. In healing, can be used to pull persistent unwanted influences out of the energy field — best used in conjunction with rose quartz, which will soothe any rawness that might result.

Work:A polished malachite sphere, obelisk or pyramid would bring a good energy to a work desk, protecting against harmful radiation as well as bringing balance and insight.

Elixir: Good protection against VDU radiation leakage. Inspires and helps re-balance burnt-out healers.

Peridot (olivine)
Hardness: 6½–7, Specific Gravity: 3.2–4.2, Crystal System: Orthorhombic

Peridot crystals are usually olive or bottle green, yellow-green or brownish in colour and are popular in jewellery. While they occur widely, some of the best gem-quality stones come from Burma, Sri Lanka, the USA, Norway, Russia and Zebirget (Egypt), an island in the Red Sea. **Olivine** refers to the continuous series of crystals from **fosterite** to **fayalite**, of which peridot is the name for gem-quality fayalite. They form in igneous rocks rich in magnesium and iron. The properties of the crystal, specific gravity, fusing point etc. vary according to its iron content.

Home: Use to treat the liver and adrenals, to free the mind of envy and to create emotional stability. According to Rudolf Steiner it activates physical and spiritual sight. It is detoxifying and tissue regenerating, bringing increased vigour and enthusiasm to mind and body.

Work: Stimulates self-worth and generosity towards co-workers. Relaxes tension and personality clashes.

Elixir: Treats envy. Brings emotional relaxation.

BLUE AND TURQUOISE STONES

Aquamarine (Beryl group)

Hardness: 7½–8, Specific Gravity: 2.7, Crystal System: Hexagonal

Found world-wide, but some large gem-quality stones come from Burma, Sri Lanka, the USA, Norway, Russia and Zebirget (Egypt), an island in the Red Sea. The name derives from Latin and means 'water from the sea' and, perhaps because of this, sailors traditionally carried aquamarine for good luck. The stone varies in colour from pale blue to light green. The bluer the crystal the more highly prized the stone, although light blue crystals can be heated to deepen their colour. It is distinguished from topaz and spinel by its lustre and lack of grey or violet hue.

Home: Aquamarine is serene and cooling. It helps to banish fears and phobias. Useful for detoxifying the body and reducing fluid retention.

Work: Helpful in combating effects of flying and motion sickness, as well as fear of flying.

Elixir: Inspires and stimulates creativity and self-expression. Results are amplified when combined with turquoise.

Blue Lace Agate (Quartz group)
Hardness: 6½–7, Specific Gravity: 2.6, Crystal System: Hexagonal
Most important deposits are found in India, Brazil and Uruguay, but it is also found in quantity in the USA, Canada, Germany and Russia. Blue lace agate is a soft blue variety of the extensive agate family, a banded microcrystalline quartz variety of chalcedony. Agate is often dyed for decorative purposes.
Home: Helpful in easing arthritis and for strengthening nails, teeth and bones. Soothes sore or strained eyes. Suits gentle people. Brings a high spiritual connection.
Work: Promotes clear thought and eases eye strain resulting from close work such as sewing, design or for those constantly using a computer screen.
Elixir: Add to the bath for a gentle reviving soak. Use gem water as a cotton wool compress on closed lids to relieve tired eyes.

Chrysocolla
Hardness: 2–4 (Peru has the hardest), Specific Gravity: 2.2, Crystal System: Monoclinic
Found in Cornwall, Australia, Italy, Bavaria, Siberia, Morocco, the USA, South America and Zimbabwe, chrysocolla is distinctively bluish-green in colour. It grows in seams or crusts in the oxidation zones of copper deposits. Its name originates from the Greek for gold, *chrysos*, and *kolla*, meaning 'glue', because it looked similar to a material used as a gold solder. It is softer than turquoise.

Home: Enhances metabolism, strengthens lungs and thyroid and helps prevent digestive problems, ulcers and arthritis. Good for female disorders and for activating feminine qualities. Cleanses subconscious thought patterns that might be blocking emotional growth and development. Eases heartache and renews emotional strength and confidence. Brings an atmosphere of stability and harmony.

Work: Promotes harmony at work and purifies the environment. Good for empowering all creative work, enabling a clear expression of ideas.

Garden: Brings greater understanding to the gardener of the best methods for nurturing health, growth and harmony in the garden and how to respect the underlying spiritual forces at work.

Elixir: Add spring water as a spray to cleanse any environment, especially where there have been emotional upsets or disturbances.

Fluorite (Halite group)

Hardness: 4, Specific Gravity: 3.3, Crystal System: Cubic

Fluorite is extremely widespread and very fine examples are known from many areas including the USA, Canada, Mexico, Germany, Norway, Sweden and Russia. Also many areas of the United Kingdom including the Yorkshire Dales, the Derbyshire Peaks (main source of **Blue John**), the Mendips, Cumbria, north Wales and Cornwall. The cubic shape and octahedral cleavage of fluorite crystals is distinctive. They form in hydrothermal mineral veins and occur as transparent or in a great variety of colours ranging from deep purple, pink and blue to green and yellow, depending on the elements bound into the crystal structure. Fluorite is an important component in the chemical industry. Exposure to blue or indigo light for 30 minutes amplifies its properties. *Home*: Fluorite is strengthening to the teeth and bones and assists in the absorption of nutrients. Especially useful if worn close to tooth enamels, e.g. as ear-rings. Eases pneumonia and viral inflammation and can dispel at the onset symptoms of colds, flu', strep' and staph' infections, herpes, ulcers etc. The influence is grounding, improving the assimilation of life force energy from the etheric into the physical body. Helps concentration and meditation. Works with *chakras* according to colour.

Work: Relieves anxiety and balances the plus and minus polarities of the mind. Increases electrical charge to the brain, improving concentration and raising IQ. Used on the brow *chakra*, it brings higher wisdom to see the reality behind the illusion and create a centred space in the midst of activity.

Elixir: For anxiety, stress and sexual frustration. Improves the assimilation of all minerals. Use in the bath to ease arthritic conditions.

Kyanite
Hardness: 6–7 across cleavage planes, 4–5 along them, Specific Gravity: 3.6, Crystal System: Triclinic
Kyanite crystals occur in aluminium-rich metamorphic rock and are widely distributed with good examples found in Brazil, Austria, Switzerland, France, Sri Lanka, India, Kenya, Australia and the USA. They are used commercially for making specialised high-temperature and acid-resistant porcelain products, as they are not able to be fused or dissolved in acid. Crystals are white, grey, light blue or greenish in colour with perfect cleavage in two directions. Fragile and delicate — handle with care. Due to solubility and aluminium content, not suitable for use as an elixir.

Home: Kyanite is especially good for throat problems. Lifts depression, shifts negative attitudes and oppressive influences.

Work: Kyanite enhances the voice of singers and orators and generally benefits creative expression. Qualities of loyalty, trust, devotion, reliability and serenity are enhanced by this crystal.

Turquoise

Hardness: 5–6, Specific Gravity: 2.8, Crystal System: Triclinic

From the French, meaning 'Turkish stone', historically turquoise was often mined in Iran, then came to Europe via Turkey, and so was thought to originate there. It is still found in Iran today as well as in Tibet, France, Chile and the USA. Turquoise is sacred to the Pueblo Indians of New Mexico. Usually opaque bright to light blue or greenish blue, turquoise was originally not thought to be crystalline until crystals were found in 1911 in Virginia, USA. Normally found as massive or nodular aggregates, the formation of turquoise is due to alterations in aluminium-rich igneous and sedimentary rocks. Avoid bleach or chlorine. Fades in sunlight.

Home: Turquoise was used in ancient Egypt for cataracts and eye troubles. It protects against environmental pollution, especially background radiation, promoting a long and healthy life. Physically toning and emotionally calming. Its high copper content makes it a fine energy conductor, vitalising the blood, toning the body and assisting tissue regeneration.

Work: Traditionally thought to strengthen work animals and to change colour to warn its wearer of danger. Great protection against background radiation at work. Worn at the throat, it will enhance communication and gifts of speech. Best set in silver.

Elixir: Protects against environmental pollution. Promotes the efficient absorption of nutrients as well as general health and well-being.

Sapphire (Corundum group)
Hardness: 9, Specific Gravity: 3.9–4.1, Crystal System: Hexagonal
From the Latin *sapphirus*, meaning 'blue', although sapphires can also be violet, green, pink or yellow, depending on varying traces of iron, titanium, vanadium or chrome within the stone, sapphires are found in Montana (USA), Kashmir (India), Australia, Brazil, Burma, Cambodia, Thailand and central and eastern Africa. Kashmiri sapphires are characteristically pure, cornflower blue; those from Sri Lanka are patchy blue; and Australian sapphires are deep blue with a greenish-blue reflection. Heat treatment is very common and difficult to detect, except in a magnified cross-section. Thailand controls the market as the major processor of sapphires in the world.
Home: The Buddhists say that sapphire inspires prayer, devotion and spiritual enlightenment. It is widely associated with truth and wisdom and is thought to balance desire and passion with divine inspiration. The three points within a star sapphire are said to represent destiny, faith and hope, so this gem is particularly associated with granting wishes. Sapphire is also good for the pituitary gland and, therefore, the whole glandular system, the heart and the kidneys. Aids dream recall.
Work: The stone is associated with awakening psychic gifts and bringing inspiration and clarity to communication. Brings luck and helps the realisation of dreams. Helpful for those involved in religious service or participating in ceremonial or public office.

INDIGO AND VIOLET STONES
Amethyst (Quartz group)
Hardness: 7, Specific Gravity: 2.63-2.65, Crystal System: Hexagonal

Spectacular examples of amethyst are found in Minas Gerais, Brazil, but large quantities are also found in Australia, India, Sri Lanka, Russia, Madagascar, South Africa, Czechoslovakia, the USA and Canada. Amethyst derives its name from the Greek *amethustos* which means 'not drunk', as it was believed the wearer of this stone was protected from the effects of alcohol.

The most precious of the quartz group of crystals and highly prized as a gemstone, its value dropped when large deposits were found in Brazil and Uruguay at the end of the nineteenth century. These violet, purple or pink crystals always grow from a base. The colouring is due to traces of iron which are distributed in varying bands distinguishing amethyst from other similar crystals. Uruguay is famed for small, dark purple crystals growing from a banded agate matrix instead of a malachite base, as with other sources of amethyst.

Home: Strengthens the immune and endocrine systems. Very powerful energiser and blood cleanser. Positively affects right brain activity and the pituitary and pineal glands. Representing the violet ray of alchemical transformation, it enhances psychism, aids meditation and gives strong protection when worn. Treats and breaks links in addiction. A great aura cleanser, it is ideal placed at the entrance to the home where it positively influences all who pass.

Work: Powerful protection against background radiation. Assists concentration and all mental activity. Particularly helpful when studying.

Elixir: Brings balance, integration and confidence. Enhances intuition and assists meditation.

Ametrine (Quartz group)
Hardness: 7, Specific Gravity: 2.63–2.65, Crystal System: Hexagonal
Unusual form of amethyst combined with citrine — a very high energy that lifts and clears oppressive conditions. (See properties listed for both, in addition.)
Home: Brings equilibrium to opposing forces — useful in circumstances where there is a need to balance the different needs of family members. Brings harmony and a highly spiritual consciousness. Disperses negativity and releases energy blockages from the aura and the environment. Inspires awareness of the connectedness of life.
Work: Clears attitudes of discrimination and prejudice, enhancing compatibility and appreciation of each person's special gifts for the benefit of all.
Elixir: Helpful for easing transitions and physical changes such as puberty, menopause and surgery (transplants, artificial organs etc.).

Azurite
Hardness: 3½–4, Specific Gravity: 3.7–3.9, Crystal System: Monoclinic
Azurite is a secondary copper ore from which azure (blue) pigment was first derived. Also known as **chessylite**, it is found in Chessy (France), Greece, Australia, Iran, Namibia, Mexico and Chile. It forms at lower temperatures than malachite, which it can turn into through ion exchange in moisture. Crystals are usually azure-blue but can also be dark blue with a hint of green. They are relatively soft with a vitreous lustre. Powdered azurite will become greenish in time as it turns to malachite.
Home: Because of its copper content, azurite enhances the energy flow through the nervous system. It strengthens the

blood and helps the body to utilise oxygen and can also ease arthritis and spinal problems. It is purifying to the mental body and greatly enhances meditation.

Work: Inspires creativity and helps cut through illusion.

Elixir: For expansion of consciousness, especially in healers. Use a few drops in the bath to ease depression.

Labradorite ('Merlin stone') (Feldspar group)

Hardness: 6-6½, Specific Gravity: 2.6-2.75, Crystal System: Triclinic

Very large specimens come from Labrador (Canada) where it gets its name. It is also found in Finland, Madagascar, Japan, Mexico and the USA. Labradorite is distinctive for its iridescent peacock blue, green and purple colours, which are displayed when light strikes it, especially on a polished surface. The effect is probably due to the play of light on the twinned layers of the cleavage surface. It is a plagioclase which is one of the essential minerals in igneous rocks. Labradorite is used for decorative ornaments, small boxes, brooches, beads and other jewellery.

Home: Beneficial to the nerves, brain, pineal and pituitary glands, the liver and the lymphatic system, labradorite is also helpful in balancing and stabilising the movement of life force/sexual energy (*kundalini*) in the body. It enhances meditation and telepathy and increases inspiration, intuition, imagination and discernment. Helps ability to see auras and good for those with poor physical sight. Protects the aura and encourages peaceful sleep.

Work: Brings inspiration and imagination to transform stale attitudes and conditions. Encourages the flow of fresh ideas and new energy.

Elixir: For unrealistic expectations and frustrated desires.

Lapis Lazuli

Hardness: 5-6, Specific Gravity: 2.4-2.9, Crystal System: Cubic

Lapis lazuli is a rare, usually massive, composite mineral found in marbles which are made by contact metamorphism. The name derives from the Latin *lapis*, 'stone', and the Arabic *azul*, meaning 'blue'. Found in Afghanistan, Russia, Burma, Italy, Chile, Canada and the USA, this rich blue ornamental stone is often sprinkled with gold-coloured iron pyrites. In medieval times it was powdered and used as a pigment similar to the 'ultramarine' pigment made today, but from synthetic stone. In ancient times lapis lazuli was used to relieve ague, fever, blood disorders, eye problems, neuralgia and spasms. Edgar Cayce said it imparts a sense of strength, vitality and virility.

Home: It is good for enhancing psychic abilities, spiritual contact and for strengthening the skeletal system. Often referred to as the stone of true friendship.

Work: Brings greater personal confidence and improves effective communication. Strengthens and supports in stressful circumstances.

Elixir: Valuable detoxifier. Encouraging to shy, introverted types. Helps self-expression and the release of buried emotions.

Sodalite

Hardness: 5½-6, Specific Gravity: 2.2, Crystal System: Cubic

Found in Brazil, Bolivia, Greenland, Russia, Burma, India, Canada, the USA, Romania, Portugal, Italy and Norway, sodalite is often confused with the rarer lapis lazuli because of its blue colour and because it can also contain iron pyrites. Sodalite forms in alkaline igneous rocks and silica-deficient lavas and the crystals are usually massive, from blue to violet and white to grey. The white patches are usually caused by calcite. It is named for its sodium content which makes it easily fusible. It has qualities similar to those of lapis lazuli.

Home: Stimulates the thyroid and boosts the metabolism generally. It also aids the pancreas and the lymphatic system. The most 'grounded' of the indigo stones, it balances, calms and clears the mind, removing illusion and fear. Can facilitate access to the sacred laws of the universe, stimulating thought and a calm inner 'knowing'. It encourages truthfulness in emotions, allowing the recognition and expression of true feelings.

Work: It supports direction and purpose with a lightness of heart. Sodalite is very good for those who are overly sensitive.

Elixir: Eases conflicts between conscious and subconscious impulses. Relieves fearfulness and guilt. Promotes friendship, courage, self-esteem, trust (of self and others) and endurance.

WHITE, PINK AND RUTILATED STONES
Silver

Hardness: 2½–3, Specific Gravity: 9.6–11, Crystal System: Cubic

Silver crystals are rare but can occur, soft and wire-like, in hydrothermal veins. It more usually takes the form of irregular masses in the oxidised zones of ore deposits. Locations include the USA, Canada, Mexico, Chile, Norway, Germany, the United Kingdom and Australia. This inert, silvery-white precious metal was called 'tears of the moon' by the Incas and is used extensively today in jewellery, electronics, dentistry and photography, because silver bromide is light sensitive. It is soft, malleable and tarnishes quickly.

Home: In Western medicine silver nitrate has been used as an eye wash, to treat burns and rhinitis. Silver has been used, among other things, to fill teeth, replace bones and joints and treat ear, nose, throat, rectal, urethral and vaginal inflammations and warts. But too much silver in the body can be damaging. Silver is an excellent energy conductor and facilitates change and transformation. Related to the moon, the feminine and the subconscious, it assists communication with the higher self. Silver is enhanced by exposing it to the light of a full or new moon.

Work: Brings refinement, sensitivity and inspiration.

Elixir: Treats nervous stress. Enhances the intellect and feminine qualities.

Celestite

Hardness: 3–3½, Specific Gravity: 3.9, Crystal System: Orthorhombic

The first celestite crystals found were a celestine blue, after which they were named. Other crystals are colourless or white with bluish zones. The finest quality crystals have been found in Madagascar, England, Tunisia, Sicily and Lake Erie (USA). The main source of strontium, which is used to make signal flares and fireworks, its colour when powdered and burned is bright crimson. Crystals are translucent or transparent with a pearly lustre and are slightly water soluble.

Home: Healing properties include stress reduction and stimulation of the thyroid function. This exquisite stone helps you to access your unique gifts and potential by increasing a conscious connection between the divine, the higher self and the everyday mind.

Work: The stone brings peace of mind, clarity of thought and speech and enhanced creative expression. Assists in heightening awareness to finer vibrations. Ideal for those connected with the arts, especially music.

Elixir: Eliminates toxins, balancing outside forces and transmuting chaos and pain in the aura into love and light.

Diamond

Hardness: 10, Specific Gravity: 3.5, Crystal System: Cubic

From the Greek *adamas*, meaning 'invincible', diamonds are formed in the depths of the earth, then blasted towards the surface by volcanic forces as pure crystallised carbon. Found in Australia (largest production), South Africa, Russia, Arkansas (USA), Brazil, Venezuela, Ghana, Angola and Zaire, diamond seams run as deep as 200 km, so the surface is only scratched by mines that run to a depth of 1–2 km. They are the hardest of all crystals and this, combined with their brilliant sparkle (due to high refractivity), makes them uniquely desirable. Diamonds are usually colourless, black, grey, brownish or green. Very rarely they occur in colours such as blue, red, yellow or violet.

Home: It is a master healer, purifying the physical and etheric bodies and enhancing the full spectrum of energies in the whole being. It is associated with abundance, purity, innocence and faithfulness and is believed to be a powerful protection against negative thoughts. Some care should be taken as the exceptionally strong energy radiated by diamond can overpower or drain personal energy.

Work: Diamond enhances brain function and is traditionally associated with strengthening the mind due to its hardness.

Kunzite (Spodumene group)

Hardness: 6–7, Specific Gravity: 3.2, Crystal System: Monoclinic

Formed in granite pegmatites, this rose-pink or light violet crystal is named after the turn of the century gemologist,

George Frederick Kunz, who first described it. Kunzite crystals are normally long and prismatic with uneven terminations and show different depths of colour when viewed from different directions. Kunzite is mined for its lithium content and it is also cut into gemstones. Fine examples come from Madagascar, Brazil and the USA. Lithium is used in medicine to treat a large range of illnesses from alcoholism to Parkinson's disease and mental disorders.

Home: Kunzite is useful in treating addictive behaviour and depressive conditions. It balances the cardio-vascular system at a physical and cellular level and assists general tissue regeneration. It helps to increase the flow of life force into the physical body. The energy of this crystal is enhanced if placed under the colour red for about fifteen minutes.

Elixir: Assists in breaking addictive behaviour and in re-aligning the subtle bodies.

Morganite (Beryl group)
Hardness: 7½–8, Specific Gravity: 2.8–2.9, Crystal System: Hexagonal

Named after the American banker and mineral collector J. P. Morgan, morganite is a pink or rose-pink form of **beryl** which forms in masses or as prismatic crystals. Heat-treated, morganite turns into **aquamarine**. Important deposits are found in the Minas Gerais region of Brazil, Madagascar, Mozambique, Namibia, Zimbabwe and California.

Home:Activates and cleanses the heart *chakra*, bringing love and growth into all relationships. Carries far memories of historical times past that may be recovered in meditation and during sleep. Releases pent-up emotions and clears inner conflicts with love and understanding. Promotes empathy.

Work: Brings wisdom, creativity, self-control and love to all
actions. Facilitates a reverence for life and listening with, and
speaking from the heart.
Garden: Morganite brings a better understanding and love of
the earth which can be expressed through harmony and love
in your garden.

Rose Quartz (Quartz group)
Hardness: 7, Specific Gravity: 2.65, Crystal System: Hexagonal
The rose-pink colour of this crystal is caused by traces of
titanium or manganese in the quartz. Rose quartz is fairly
common in its massive form, but high-quality crystals are
found in the USA, Brazil, Madagascar and Japan. Its lovely
colour makes it a prized ornamental stone, although it is
somewhat brittle and difficult to work. Well-formed crystals
are rare and flat-sided crystals were only found as recently as
1981 in Brazil. Rose quartz tends to be milky rather than
transparent and loses its colour when heated.
Home and work: Like all quartz crystals, rose quartz is *good
protection against background radiation*. Wonderful for all
conditions where love, gentleness and balance are needed.
Long associated with the heart and beauty, the 'love stone' is
an excellent and gentle healer. It will ease fear, guilt, jealousy,
anger and resentment. A positive influence on the kidneys
and the circulation, as well as increasing fertility, rose quartz
is useful for blood disorders and most sexually related
illnesses. Very good for the skin and restoring a youthful com-
plexion. Excellent as a general nurturer for children, it will
ease nightmares and bring restful sleep. Use as part of a travel
pack (see Chapter 10).
Garden: Rose quartz is equally beneficial in the garden. Use
as a spray or placed alongside sick plants. Also outstanding

for creating a special atmosphere of love and beauty (see suggestions in the gardening section).

Elixir: Brings a life-enhancing awareness of beauty, self-responsibility and optimism. Rose quartz gem water as an atomiser or face wash is good for promoting clear, soft and youthful skin.

Selenite (Gypsum)

Hardness: 2, Specific Gravity: 2.35, Crystal System: Monoclinic

Selenite is the clear, transparent form of **gypsum**. (Rosette-shaped masses of gypsum with a lot of sand in them are called **desert roses** and the granular form is known as **alabaster**.) It is very soft and can be scratched with a fingernail. The long, tabular crystals often display swallowtail twinning. Gypsum is used in the manufacture of plaster of paris (where it is mined extensively) and for fine white plasterwork. The most common sulphate mineral, it is also a fertiliser and is used in glass-making. Selenite is extensively mined in the United Kingdom, Russia, France and the USA. Very fine crystals have been found in Chile, Mexico, the USA and Sicily, and high-quality clusters were discovered in Madagascar in 1995.

Home: As the homoeopathic remedy, *calcarea sulphurica,* it is used to treat mucous discharges, skin eruptions, glandular swelling and problems with the tongue. Selenite is good for strengthening teeth and bones and for restoring elasticity to the skin, tissue regeneration and rejuvenating the prostate, testicles and uterus. The energy is soothing and grounding. Its influence is visionary and light enhancing, freeing the body and mind of unwanted conditions.

Work: Helpful in cases of light sensitivity. Place within your aura for clarity and strength. Brings focus, growth and luck to business ventures.

Sugilite

Also known as **royal lazel** or **luvulite**. Found mainly in the Kalahari Desert of South Africa, this violet-pink stone earths the violet/magenta rays and is associated with the pituitary and pineal glands and the spiritualisation of matter. Balances the hemispheres of the brain, improving physical co-ordination, vision and balance.

Home: Draws out toxins, deep-rooted conditions and emotional blocks. It absorbs and dissolves anger. Very protective, it assists with self-acceptance, forgiveness, belief in self and trust in life, making it an ideal stone to work with in healing and psychotherapy. Cleanses the aura, relieves depression and brings peace of mind. Also relieves physical headaches.

Work: Eliminates all conditions of hostility — prejudice, anger, jealousy, insensitivity and mistrust — helping to bring peace, stability and acceptance. Promotes the art of living in the present moment, making it conscious and the best you can — thereby creating a better future.

Calcite

Hardness: 3, Specific Gravity: 2.7, Crystal System: Hexagonal
Found world-wide, although exceptionally fine crystals have come from the United Kingdom, Iceland and Czechoslovakia, calcite is formed by the evaporation of calcium-rich solutions. Usually colourless, transparent, slightly milky pearl or pinkish-white, but also found (as masses) in colours — use coloured calcites with appropriate *chakras*. Clear crystals were once used as prisms. Compact masses of calcite such as lime and cement are used for building and also in the manufacture of fertilisers and chemicals. An energy amplifier, calcite also releases electrical impulses under pressure (the

piezo-electric effect). **Iceland spar** — optical quality calcite — has the property of double refraction.

Home: In healing, this stone assists in balancing the male/female polarities. Aids kidney function and balances the assimilation of calcium in the body. It reduces stress, grounds excess energy and inspires a sense of lightness and joy. It increases abilities in astral projection.

Work: Brings lightness and clarity to the workplace and greater strength and energy to the aura. Clear calcite will amplify all the *chakras* and can be used for *chakra* balancing. Excellent for bringing illumination and understanding to study of all sorts.

Garden: Spray as a gem water to energise the whole garden or to boost specific plants. Excellent for promoting healthy growth in vegetables.

Elixir: Use in the bath as an energiser.

Moonstone (Adularia) (Feldspar group)
Hardness: 6–6½, Specific Gravity: 2.6, Crystal System: Monoclinic
Named after its moon-like pearly lustre, moonstone is a prized gem found in Australia, Burma, Sri Lanka, India, Tanzania and the USA. It is a low-temperature form of **orthoclase** which is common in many igneous rocks. Moonstones are normally colourless with a pale grey or green tint, a silvery-white or blue shimmer and a mobile reflection. **Star** and **cat's-eye** moonstones are also found.

Home: Moonstone brightens at each new moon and brings lunar qualities of psychic awareness, emotional sensitivity, peace and harmony. Long used as a protection against insanity, it also relieves stress and anxiety. Very good for all female ailments, balancing the hormones and regulating the menstrual cycle. Promotes general flexibility and a willingness to 'go with the flow'.

Work: Brings greater flexibility and intuition. Enables graceful receptivity and openness to the suggestions and ideas of others.

Elixir: Good for those working out stress associated with the mother. Integrates emotions. Good for increasing sensitivity, care and attentiveness in those who tend to be overbearing or bossy. Allows acceptance of help from others.

Opal (Quartz group)

Hardness: 5½–6½, Specific Gravity: 1.9–2.5, Crystal System: None

From the Greek word *opalus* (from the Sanskrit *upala*, meaning 'precious stone') opals were mined only in Czechoslovakia until the nineteenth century when they were also found in Australia and the USA. The finest precious opals come from South Australia and New South Wales, but other sources include Mexico (particularly for **fire opals**), Guatemala, Honduras and the USA. They have no crystal structure, occurring amorphously in grape-like or stalactitic shapes within cavities and veins. The colour of opals varies from milky pale blues and pinks to almost black. They are extremely porous and gem-quality opal displays a brilliant colour play probably due to optical light refraction among the closely packed balls of silica in its structure. They can contain as much as 30 per cent water by volume, are very fragile and can crack if exposed to drying heat, salt or acidic food. Opals should be wetted regularly and stored in humid conditions.

The superstition that opals are unlucky unless you are born in October (opal is a traditional birthstone for October) originated in the nineteenth century, when they suddenly became very fashionable as a result of the new finds in Australia and America. Seeing their own market declining, and capitalising on the physical fragility of opals to enhance their reputation, the diamond industry spread the clever rumour. Thus opals instantly lost eleven-twelfths of their market success and the price of diamonds was restored.

Home: Historically, opals have been used to cure eye troubles and to improve vision. Their feminine watery nature and sensitivity connects them with intuitive gifts and inspiration. They also have a reputation for assisting women in childbirth. Opals are stimulating to the pineal and pituitary glands and are fine emotional balancers.

Work: Broadens the mind and outlook. Brings energy, spontaneity and vitality. Mirrors and amplifies feelings and brings out hidden aspects of situations.

Elixir: Increases receptivity to new ideas and outside stimuli.

Quartz (Quartz group)
Hardness: 7, Specific Gravity: 2.65, Crystal System: Hexagonal
Quartz is one of the most common minerals making up the earth's crust (12 per cent by volume) and occurs world-wide with fine-quality commercially mined crystals coming from Brazil, Arkansas (USA) and Madagascar. The Greeks believed clear quartz was water frozen by the gods to remain ice for ever and they named it *krustallos*, meaning 'ice'. Quartz crystals occur as six sided prisms terminated by six triangular faces. They are often twinned or in clusters and sometimes double terminated. There are many varieties of quartz, such as **amethyst**, **smoky**, **rose** or **citrine** (see separate entries for each of these). Much of this book is devoted to the many ways of using quartz crystals. *All quartz is good protection against background radiation.*

Clear quartz is the 'universal healer'. It has long been prized for its ability to remove negative thoughts, protect and cleanse the system, increase psychism, enhance meditation and raise consciousness. It has been used in many cultures for healing and as a link with spiritual realms. It receives, stores, activates, amplifies and transmits energy. It stimulates brain function and amplifies thought forms.
Elixir: Cleanses and protects the energy field. For rigid, inflexible attitudes, emotional extremes and hysteria.

Milky or white quartz is used in the same way as clear quartz but is generally gentler and more diffuse (some say more 'feminine'), although each crystal's healing properties and potential will vary individually.

Rutilated quartz, containing acicular rutile inclusions which often look like beautiful golden hairs within the crystal, is excellent for tissue regeneration, increasing the life force and for strengthening the immune system. It is highly electric, very powerful and more intense than clear quartz.
Elixir: Boosts mental activity and eases depression.

Herkimer diamond, found in Herkimer, New York State, is formed in double-terminated very bright, clear crystals, somewhat like diamonds. Similar crystals are also found in Mexico. It has similar qualities to clear quartz, radiating energy, drawing out toxins, releasing stress and balancing the energies of body and mind. Its radiance is enhanced if exposed to diamond. Prized in the native American tradition as a dream teacher and helper.
Elixir: Especially valuable for relieving symptoms of stress.

Aqua aura, opal aura and titania

Quartz that has been fused with gold, platinum and titanium, respectively. The molecules of the metals adhere to the natural electrical charge surrounding the quartz and cannot be rubbed off. These speciality crystals combine the properties of both. Platinum is very purifying and intense. Titanium strengthens brain activity. All are cleansing to the aura. These crystals prompt very strong reactions — you'll either love them or hate them.

Reference Notes

Chapter 1

1. Dublin: Gill & Macmillan, 1997. This and all subsequent books referred to in the text are listed in the Recommended Reading.

Chapter 6

1. Care should be taken with stones that may be soluble or even slightly toxic in water. Notes have been made under specific entries in the Directory section where there is unsuitability or specific care required in making a gem elixir.

2. You should use only gem waters when treating someone who cannot tolerate alcohol. They should be prepared fresh in each case.

3. As note 2 above.

Recommended Reading

Anderson, Mary, *Colour Healing*, Wellingborough, Northamptonshire:
The Aquarian Press, 1979

Ashcroft-Nowicki, Dolores, *Highways of the Mind*, Wellingborough,
Northamptonshire: The Aquarian Press, 1987

Attenborough, Liz, *The Children's Book of Poems, Prayers and
Meditations*, Shaftesbury, Dorset: Element Children's Books,
1998

Berne, Eric, MD, *Games People Play*, London: Penguin Books, 1964

Bloom, William, *Meditation in a Changing World*, Glastonbury:
Gothic Image, 1987

Bonewitz, Ra, *Cosmic Crystals*, Wellingborough, Northamptonshire:
The Aquarian Press, 1983

Bonewitz, Ra, *The Cosmic Crystal Spiral*, Shaftesbury, Dorset:
Element Books, 1986

Bowman, Catherine, *Crystal Awareness*, St Paul, Minnesota:
Llewellyn Publications, 1990

Brennan, Barbara Ann, *Hands of Light*, New York: Bantam Books,
1988

Brennan, Barbara Ann, *Light Emerging*, New York: Bantam Books,
1993

Brennan, J. H., *Astral Doorways*, Loughborough: Thoth Publications,
1995

Brennan, J. H., *Magic for Beginners*, Minnesota: Llewellyn, 1998

Brown, Simon, *Principles of Feng Shui*, London: Thorsens, 1996

Burgess, Jacquie, *Healing with Crystals*, Dublin: Gill & Macmillan,
1997

Butler, W. E., *How to Read the Aura*, London: The Aquarian Press,
1971

Caldecott, Moira, *Crystal Legends*, London: The Aquarian Press

Chase, Pamela and Pawlik, Jonathan, *The Newcastle Guide to Healing with Crystals* and *The Newcastle Guide to Healing with Gemstones*, North Hollywood, California: Newcastle Publishing Co., 1988 & 1989

Chopra, Deepak, *Quantum Healing*, New York: Bantam, 1989

Clarke, Ethne, *Water Features for Small Gardens*, London: Ward Lock, 1998

Darling, Peter, *Crystal Identifier*, London: The Apple Press, 1991

Dorland, Frank, *Holy Ice*, St Paul, Minnesota: Galde Press, 1992

Eliade, Mircea, *Shamanism*, London: Arkana, 1989

Feldenkrais, Moshe, *The Elusive Obvious*, New York: Harper & Row, 1981

Gardner, Joy, *Color and Crystals: A Journey Through the Chakras*, Freedom, California: The Crossing Press, 1988

Geological Museum, *Gemstones*, London: British Museum, 1987

Gienger, Michael, *Crystal Power, Crystal Healing*, London: Blandford, 1998

Gimbel, Theo, *Healing Through Colour*, Saffron Walden, Essex: C.W. Daniel, 1980

Gleick, James, *Chaos*, London: Sphere, 1988

Goldman, Jonathan, *Healing Sounds*, Shaftesbury, Dorset: Element, 1992

Goodwin, Matthew Oliver, *Numerology: The Complete Guide* (2 volumes) North Hollywood, California: Newcastle Publishing Co., 1991

Gurudas, *Gem Elixirs and Vibrational Healing*, Vols 1 & 2, Boulder, Colorado: Cassandra Press, 1985 & 1986

Gyatso, Geshe Kelsang, *A Meditation Handbook*, London: Tharpa Publications, 1990

Harner, Michael, *The Way of the Shaman*, New York: Bantam Books, 1982

Harrison, Stephanie and Kleiner, Barbara, *The Crystal Wisdom Kit*, London: Piatkus, 1997

Harrison, Stephanie and Kleiner, Barbara, *Crystal Wisdom for Love*, London: Connection, 1998

Harrison, Stephanie and Kleiner, Barbara, *Crystal Wisdom for Prosperity*, London: Connection, 1998

Harrison, Stephanie and Kleiner, Barbara, *Crystal Wisdom for Health*, Boston, USA: Journey Editions, 1998

Harrison, Stephanie and Kleiner, Barbara, *Crystal Wisdom for Personal Growth*, Boston, USA: Journey Editions, 1998

Harrison, Stephanie and Tim, *New Perspective: Crystal Therapy*, Shaftesbury, Dorset: Element, 2000

Hodgson, Joan, *The Stars and the Chakras*, Liss: White Eagle Publishing Trust, 1990

Holbeche, Soozi, *The Power of Gems and Crystals*, London: Piatkus, 1989

Hunt, Roland, *The Seven Keys to Colour Healing*, London: C. W. Daniel, 1971

Jay, Roni, *Sacred Gardens*, London: Thorsens, 1998

Keyte, Geoffrey, *The Mystical Crystal*, Saffron Walden, Essex: C. W. Daniel, 1993

Kozminsky, Isidore, *The Magic and Science of Jewels and Stones*, San Rafael, California: Cassandra Press, 1988

Lansdowne, Zachary F., Ph.D., *The Chakras & Esoteric Healing*, York Beach, Maine: Samuel Weiser, Inc., 1986

Mails, Thomas E., *Secret Native American Pathways*, Tulsa, Oklahoma: Council Oak Books, 1995

Matthews, Caitlin, *Singing the Soul Back Home*, Shaftesbury, Dorset: Element, 1995

Matthews, John, *The Celtic Shaman*, Shaftesbury, Dorset: Element, 1991

Meadows, Kenneth, *The Medicine Way*, Shaftesbury, Dorset: Element, 1990

Melody, *Love is in the Earth* (3 volumes), Wheat Ridge, Colorado: Earth-Love Publishing House, 1993

Mercer, Ian, *Crystals*, London: Natural History Museum Publications

Michell, John, *The View over Atlantis*, London: Abacus, 1973

Moore, Thomas, *Care of the Soul*, London: Piatkus, 1992

Moore, Thomas, *The Re-enchantment of Everyday Life*, London: Piatkus, 1996

Morgan, Marlo, *Mutant Message Down Under*, London: HarperCollins, 1994

Myss, Caroline, Ph.D., *Anatomy of the Spirit*, London: Bantam Books, 1997

O'Donaghue, John, *Anam Cara*, London: Bantam Press, 1997

O'Donaghue, John, *Eternal Echoes*, London: Bantam Press, 1998

Oldfield, Harry and Coghill, Roger, *The Dark Side of the Brain*, Shaftesbury, Dorset: Element Books, 1988

Palmer, Magda, *The Healing Power of Crystals*, London: Rider, 1988

Park, Glen, *The Art of Changing*, Bath: Ashgrove Press, 1989

Pellant, Chris, *Rocks, Minerals & Fossils of the World*, London: Pan Books, 1990

Pennick, Nigel, *Sacred Geometry*, London: Turnstone

Philbrick, Helen and Gregg, Richard B., *Companion Plants*, London and Dulverton: Watkins Publishing, 1967

Raphaell, Katrina, *Crystal Trilogy* (3 volumes) Santa Fe, New Mexico: Aurora Press, 1985, 1987 & 1990

Rawlings, Romy, *Healing Gardens*, London: Weidenfeld and Nicolson, 1998

Redfield, James, *The Celestine Prophesy*, London: Bantam Books, 1994

Rinpoche, Sogyal, *The Tibetan Book of Living and Dying*, London: Rider Books, 1992

Sheldrake, Rupert, *Seven Experiments that could Change the World*, London: Fourth Estate, 1995

Sherwood, Keith, *Chakra Therapy*, St Paul, Minnesota: Llewellyn Publications, 1991

Smith, Michael G., *Crystal Power*, St Paul, Minnesota: Llewellyn Publications, 1985

Smith, Michael G., *Crystal Spirit*, St Paul, Minnesota: Llewellyn Publications, 1990

Spear, William, *Feng Shui Made Easy*, London: Thorsens, 1995

Sun Bear, Wabun and Weinstock, Barry, *The Path of Power*, New York: Prentice Hall Press, 1987

Sun Bear, Wabun Wind and Shawnodese, *Dreaming with the Wheel*, New York: Fireside, 1994

Suzuki, Shunryu, *Zen Mind, Beginner's Mind*, New York and Tokyo: Weatherhill, 1970

Thurman, Robert A. F. (translator) *The Tibetan Book of the Dead*, London: The Aquarian Press, 1994

White Eagle, *Spiritual Unfoldment* (4 vols), Liss: White Eagle Publishing Trust

Wombwell, Felicity, *The Goddess Changes*, London: Mandala, HarperCollins, 1991

Acknowledgments

Thanks to Edward Byrne and Paddy at Haphazard Trading Co.,The Savage Yard, Rath, Shillelagh Road,Tullow, Co. Carlow, for the loan of slate and stone backgrounds used in the photographs and who supplied and erected the stone circle in our garden with ease, ingenuity and great good humour. Thanks to Stephanie and Tim Harrison at Everlasting Gems, 46 Lower Green Road, Esher, Surrey KT10 8HD for beautiful crystals and friendship. For many fascinating conversations and some rare crystals, my gratitude to George Peche. Thank you to Ann Maria and Claire at Chrysalis Holistic Centre, Donard, Co.Wicklow, for their warmth and support to a new girl in Ireland. To everyone at The Natural Living Centre, Walmer House, Station Road, Raheny, Dublin 5, who inspire me to spend everything I earn from the workshops in their magical shop! Last but not least, thank you to Michael Gill for his help and warm encouragement.

Further Information

For further information about courses or crystal therapy you can visit Jacquie's website:
http://homepage.eircom.net/~herbie/jackbio.html
Write to Jacquie at Slaney House, Tullow, Co. Carlow, Republic of Ireland,
or send an e-mail to: jacquie@eircom.net

Index

absent healing, 192-3
acupuncture, 80
  Kirlian photography, 82
  meridians, 55
Adams, Dr Mike, 37, 39
adularia, 251-2
agate, 219
alabaster, 249
amazonite, 229-30
amethyst, 240
amethyst bed, 30
ametrine, 241
apophyllite, 228
aqua aura, 255
aquamarine, 234-5, 247
arts, the, 126
aspect of home, 64-78
aura, personal, 53-5
  clearing, 54
Australia, 5, 15
aventurine, 228-9
azurite, 241-2

Bach Flowers Rescue Remedy,
  38-9, 105, 106
balancing
  chakras, 120-123
  personal energy, 83-4
bathroom, 74-5
Beauty Way, 156-8

bedroom, 85-7
Berne, Dr Eric, 115
Bhattacharyya, Dr Benoytosh, 9
Bible, the, 8-9
biodynamics, 129-31
Black Elk, 153, 154
black stones, 216-19
bloodstone, 230
Bloom, William, 189, 205
blue lace agate, 235
blue stones, 234-9
Borneo, 5
bornite, 28
breath cleansing, 30
breathing, 184-5
Burr, Dr Harold Saxton, 80-81
'butterfly effect,' 34-6

calcite, 250-251
California, 11
cancer, 111
car, crystals in, 102-3
carnelian, 219-20
celestite, 245-6
Celtic calendar, 162-6
centre (Tai Ch'i), 67
chakras, 55-8
  balancing exercise, 120-123
  chakra stones, 57-8
chanting, 114, 204-7

Chaos Theory, 34-6
charging, 31-2
Chase, P. and Pawlik, J., 30, 186
chessylite, 241-2
children, crystals for, 88-97
China, 140
chrysocolla, 235-6
circles. *see* sacred circles
citrine, 225-6
cleanliness, 50
  cleansing ritual, 51
clear quartz, 254
clusters, 18
Cobenos tribe, 4-5
colour directory, 211-55
colour therapy, 9
communal living, 63-78
compass test, 37-8
concentration, 119-26
confidence, crystals for, 93-7
copper, 220-221
corundum, 14
creativity, 42, 125
  visualisation, 194-202
cross-quarter grid, 39-40
crystal frequencies, 12-13,
    110-111
crystal gazing, 6-8
crystal grids, 38-9
  gardening, 137-8
crystal optics, 13
crystal systems, 213-15

crystal waters, 137
crystallo-luminescence, 113-14
crystals
  caring for, 24-32
  choice of, 16-23
    with the heart, 21-2
  constituents of, 211-13
  directory of, 211-55
  healing tradition, 3-9
  in the home, 47-8
  life improvement, 33-46
  physical properties of, 10-15
Curtis, Natalie, 208

dedication, 31-2
delicate crystals, 28-9
desert roses, 249
diamond, 246
dioptase, 231-2
divination, 6-8
dowsing, 22-3
dreamcatcher, 92-3, 177
dreams, 173-9
  crystals, 176
  lucid dreaming, 178-9
  protecting dream space,
    176-7
  remembering, 174-6
  visualisation, 177-8
  working with, 173-4
dreamtime, entering, 201-2

eating area, 73-4
Eckhart, Meister, 186
eight directions, 64-7
electrical field radiation, 36-9
electromagnetic fields
    health risks, 111-14
    workplace, 110-11
emerald, 232
energy, personal
    balancing, 51-3, 83-4
    boosting, 54-5
    mapping, 55-8
energy fields
    personal, 53-5, 79-81
energy transformation, 13
energy vampires, 114-15
environment, 26-7
    of home, 64-78
essential oils, 105-6

'faith healing,' 7
feng shui, 47, 99. *see also*
    home environment
    eight directions, 64-7
fluorite, 236-7
form, effects of, 20-21
foundations, 67-8
fractal geometry, 33-4
Francis, St, 45
Freud, Sigmund, 173
frustration, 102

gardening, biodynamic, 129-38
    ailing plants, 138
    companion crystals, 136-7
    companion planting, 132-6
    planetary influences,
        130-131
gardens, 139-52
garnet, 221-2
gem elixirs, 58-61
gem remedies, 8
gem waters, 58-61
geodes, 18
geopathic stress, 36-7, 39-46
Gienger, Michael, 27
gold, 225
gold stones, 225-8
gold tiger eye, 226-7
Goodwin, Matthew, 42
Graham, Ian, 197
green stones, 228-34
Gurudas, 60
gypsum, 249

halite, 28
hallways, 71
harmony, creation of,
    120-123
Harner, Michael, 11
healing, 49-62
    absent, 192-3
    of the earth, 31
healing frame, 96-7

health risks
  electromagnetic fields,
    111-14
Hehaka Sapa, 153, 154
hematite, 217
herbs, healing, 159
Herkimer diamond, 254
Hindu energy system, 55
home
  crystals in the, 47-8
  environment, 64-78
  heart of the home ritual, 68-9

Iceland spar, 251
Inca-rose, 222-3
India, 9, 17
indigo stones, 240-244
inner journeys, 201-2
insomnia, 118
inspiration, 119-26
intuition, use of, 21-3
Ireland, 8

jade, 230-231
Japan. *see* Zen garden
jasper, 222
Jay, Roni, 143
jet-lag, 103-5
jewellery, 19-20
Johnson, Ken, 82
Julian of Norwich, Mother, 205
Jung, Carl, 40-41, 173

Kirlian photography, 81-3
kitchen, 71-3
kunzite, 246-7
kyanite, 237-8

labradorite, 242
landings, 71
lapis lazuli, 243
laser technology, 14
lemon effect, 194-5
life test, 24-5
light
  crystal optics, 13
  natural, 115-18
lithium, 10
living-room, 75-6
luvulite, 250

malachite, 232-3
Malaysia, 5
Matthews, John, 164
medicine wheel, 154-9
Medicines Act, UK, 59
meditation, 180-193
  breathing, 184-5
  creating space, 180-181
  forms of, 186-93
    absent healing, 192-3
    active attention, 186-7
    contemplation, 187
    inner wisdom, 190-192
    learning to relax, 181-4

meditation *contd.*
    sound and movement,
        203-10
Merlin stone. *see* labradorite
Mesmer, Dr, 79-80
milky quartz, 254
mirrors, 76-8
    frame, 96-7
missile technology, 14
Miwok, 11
mobile phones, 112
Mohs' Scale, 213
moonlight, charging with, 27-8
moonstone, 251-2
morganite, 247-8
morphogenic fields, 83
Moss, Thelma, 82
moss agate, 8
moving crystals, 207-8
moving meditation, 203-10
music, 112-14, 126
Myss, Dr Caroline, 53, 57

National Cancer Institute, 111
Native Americans, 6-7, 153,
    154
natural quartz point, 17-18
necklaces, 19-20
Negritos, 5
nightmares, 89-93
North America, 6-7, 29, 153,
    154

numbers
    magical, 162
    sacred, 40-46

obsidian, 217-18
Oldfield, Harry, 82-3
olivine, 233-4
opal, 252-3
opal aura, 255
orange stones, 219-25
orthoclase, 251-2
overtone chanting, 206-7

pain relief, 58
Park, Glen, 121
past, release of, 198-200
peach stones, 219-25
pendants, 19-20
pendulum exercise, 22-3
peridot, 233-4
personal space, 79-87
pets, crystals for, 62
phones, portable, 112
photography, Kirlian, 81-3
piezo-electricity, 11
pink stones, 244-55
planet, crystal, 15
planetary influences
    gardening, 130-131
plants, 110
pocket friends, 95-6
polarity, discovering, 52-3

power socket radiation, 36-9
prayers, for sleep, 89-92
prosperity, 124-5
protection, 50-51
pyramids, 20-21
pyro-electricity, 12

quartz
 choice of, 16
 description of, 253-5
quiet room, 87

radio transmission, 12-13
rainbow collections, 96-7
rebalancing, 36
red stones, 219-25
Redfield, James, 114
reflexology zones, 19
refractive index, 13
Reich, Wilhelm, 80
Reichenbach, Baron von, 80
relationship, importance of,
 25-6
releasing the past, 198-200
rhodochrosite, 222-3
rose quartz, 248-9
rough stones, 18
royal lazel, 250
ruby, 224-5
Russia, 15
rutilated quartz, 254
rutilated stones, 244-55

sacred circles, 153-69
 Irish stone circle, 159-61
 spiral maze, 166-9
 tree circle, 165-6
sacred numbers, 40-46
sacred spiral walk, 209-10
sapphire, 239
Scotland, 8
Seasonal Affective Disorder
 (SAD), 115-18
selenite, 249
Senoi dream system, 89, 173-4
shamans, 17, 31
 power of, 4-5
Sheldrake, Rupert, 83
shift work, 118
Sick Building Syndrome, 99,
 108-10
silicon chips, 14
silver, 244-5
six pointed star, 44-6
sleep, 89-93
smoky quartz, 218-19
smudging, 29-30
snowflake obsidian, 217-18
sodalite, 243-4
soul retrieval, 5-6
sound
 effects of, 112-14
 vibrations, 204
South America, 4-5
spheres, 20

spiral maze, 166-9
spirals of transformation, 208-10
stairs, 71
Star of David, 44-6
'star people,' 9
Steiner, Rudolph, 129-31
study area, 87
studying, 123-4
success, 124-5
sugilite, 250
sunlight, charging with, 27-8
synthetic crystals, 14

talc, 28
talisman, 95-6
thresholds, 70-71
tiger eye, 226-7
titania, 255
Tomatis, Dr Alfred, 113
topaz, 227-8
tourmaline, 216-17
travel kit, 103
travel sickness, 106-7
travelling, 101-7
tree circle, 165-6
trust in life, 119-20
tumbled stones, 18-19
turquoise, 238-9
turquoise stones, 234-9

Vedas, 9
vesselling, 197-8

vibrational healing, 8
violet stones, 240-244
visualisation, 194-202

water features
indoor, 78
outdoor, 144-5, 149
water soluble crystals, 28
Watson, Lyall, 80
white quartz, 254
white stones, 244-55
words of power, 84-5
workplace, 108-18
WorkSafe Western Australia, 109
World Health Organisation, 108-9

yellow stones, 225-8
yoga, 80

Zen garden, 139-52
crystals, 149-52
dark mirror, 149
plants, 145-6
prayer stones, 146-7
rainbow bridge, 148
shrine, 147-8
space, 142-3
stones, 143-4
water, 144-5, 149
zero point energy, 79-80